Never Ceasing
God's Faithfulness in Grief

Kim Nolywaika

The LORD is my strength and my shield; my heart trusted in him, and I am helped: therefore my heart greatly rejoiceth; and with my song will I praise him. Psalm 28:7

TOP BUNK PRESS

Copyright © 2021 by Kim Nolywaika.

All rights reserved. No part of this publication may be reproduced, distributed or transmitted in any form or by any means, including photocopying, recording, or other electronic or mechanical methods, without the prior written permission of the publisher, except in the case of brief quotations embodied in critical reviews and certain other noncommercial uses permitted by copyright law. For permission requests, write to the address below.

Top Bunk Press
P.O. Box 237
Nenana, Alaska 99760
www.youcantrusthim.com

Scripture quotations are from the King James Version of the Holy Bible.

Cover photo: Hans Nolywaika

Never Ceasing: God's Faithfulness in Grief
Kim Nolywaika. -- 1st ed. 2021
RELIGION / Christian Living / Death, Grief, Bereavement
ISBN 978-1-7378628-2-6 (epub)
ISBN 978-1-7378628-1-9 (Kindle)
ISBN 978-1-7378628-0-2 (paperback)

Contents

1 WHAT HAPPENED	9
2 JOYSORROW	22
3 CALLED	25
4 THE FACTS	31
5 TRAINWRECK	34
6 RACKET	38
7 OLD YELLER TRUCK	41
8 TENACIOUS	44
9 LIGHT SHOW	47
10 FOUR	50
11 COMPELLED	52
12 NEW FRIENDS	54
13 WELL SAID	55
14 WHAT HANS BELIEVED	58
15 TRUSTING GOD WITH YOUR CHILD'S ETERNITY	63
16 THE BUTTERFLY	68
17 BETTER THAN A HIGH FIVE	71
18 FEARLESS	73
19 DESIRES OF A MOTHER'S HEART	75
20 HANS'S FAVORITE HYMN	77
21 HOME	79
22 TIME, THE ENEMY?	81
23 PRECIOUS	84
24 BAUBLES AND TRINKETS	87
25 CHRISTMAS PRAYER	91

26 VERIFIED	92
27 COURAGEOUS	94
28 THOUGHTS ON PSALM 84	97
29 CLEANING HOUSE	103
30 ACCIDENT OR APPOINTMENT?	107
31 MAMA	115
32 "I'LL BE RIGHT BACK."	117
33 BLIND-SIDED AT SEARS	119
34 THOUGHTS ON PSALM 55	121
35 DETESTABLE TO THE LORD	125
36 LOOKING FORWARD	128
37 THINGS ARE NOT WHAT THEY SEEM	130
38 LETTER TO A FRIEND	134
39 THE CRUX OF THE MATTER	136
40 ANGRY AT GOD	137
41 EMPTY STALLS, EMPTY BEDS	142
42 WHAT IS THIS THING CALLED FAITH?	144
43 THOUGHTS ON PSALM 105:1-5	147
44 FIRST ANNIVERSARY	149
45 CHILD LOSS: WHY WE ARE UNCOMFORTABLE	152
46 ON PRAYER	155
47 GRIEF BRAIN? ME?	160
48 GOD MEANT IT UNTO GOOD	162
49 TRUST GOD? WHY SHOULD I?	165
50 GOD'S PROMISE: PSALM 49:15	168
51 SURVIVAL IS THE STARTING POINT	170
52 WHY THE GRIEVING SHOULD GO TO CHURCH	172

53 WHY RELIGION DOESN'T HELP	177
54 BETRAYED	179
55 JOB'S WIFE	182
56 THAT WOMAN	186
57 WHAT IF?	188
58 WHY?	192
59 FORGETTING	194
60 BUT GOD GOT HIS SON BACK	197
61 SUFFERING: A PERSPECTIVE	199
62 STRENGTHENED ACCORDING TO HIS WORD	202
63 AS TIME GOES BY	210
64 GRIEF: KEEPING OUR EMOTIONS IN CHECK	213
65 THE STING OF DEATH	217
66 HEALING AFTER CHILD LOSS	223
67 FOUR YEARS AFTER: SOME OF THE POSITIVES	225
68 THE APPOINTED TIME	229
69 THE NEXT CHAPTER	234
70 REMEMBERING HANS	238

*For Manfred.
Through it all, together.
Matthew 6:19-34*

*My bursting heart
must find vent at my pen.*

ABIGAIL ADAMS

1 WHAT HAPPENED

Give sorrow words; the grief that does not speak whispers the o'er-fraught heart and bids it break.

WILLIAM SHAKESPEARE

On the evening of January 11, 2016, shortly after six o'clock, our oldest son, Hans, got into his car, approached the rural two-lane highway at the end of our driveway, and drove into the path of an oncoming pickup truck. It struck Hans's car in the driver's side door, and he died at the scene within minutes. The passengers of the other vehicle were transported to the hospital, treated, and released. Our local fire/EMS department (where Hans and his older sister were volunteer medics), responded to the call. The next day, Hans would have turned twenty-one years old.

The purpose of this book is to honor the Lord Jesus Christ in our sorrow. We declare the true and living God is real, He is good, and He is worthy to be praised. We hope to be an encouragement to parents and others who are walking through the valley of bereavement, to rejoice with them that do rejoice, and to weep with them that weep.

Our desire is to remember Hans, to share those memories with others, and to draw every bit of good we can from this painful season in our lives. Our prayer is that because Hans lived, perhaps one person might be brought to a saving knowledge of Hans's Savior, The Lord Jesus Christ.

Because knowing Jesus is everything.

~~~

Sunday: January 3, 2016

Today is my birthday. I am fifty-five years old. We take our Christmas picture right after church and have some difficulty getting everyone to smile nicely all at the same time. Hans adjusts the tripod, sets the timer, and click/flash, there it is, the last photo with all of us in it. Hans has eight more days left with us.

Thursday: January 7, 2016

I had Hans home alone for the entire day. He did his thing, I did mine, and then together we watched a couple of episodes of *Perry Mason*. But later in the afternoon, he pushed his chair back and hit the "off" button on the remote. He wanted to Talk.

It was obvious he had something on his mind. He began talking about life in general, and his own life and future in particular. Mostly, I just listened as he searched for the words he wanted to say. He had trouble pinning down what was bothering him and seemed vaguely dissatisfied as he struggled for a way to express himself. He was a fledgling, not sure of which direction to fly, not sure if flying would really be all it is cracked up to be. He was having trouble mapping out a future for himself and seemed to be reluctant to leave home. He was concerned about how Manfred and I would get along without him when he left. He was homesick before he even left home.

I reminded him that, since he was no longer a boy, he would soon have new responsibilities and, as he stayed close to God, the world and his place in it would eventually make sense to him. He gave me his slow smile and said, "I'll always be a boy." He looked directly into my eyes as he said it. He stood less than two feet away. So close. We talked a long time. It was a good talk, and it was precious.

The conversation finally came back around to less weighty matters: What kind of birthday cake do you want on Tuesday? What's for dinner? We talked about church, work, cars. He made an offhand comment about pickup trucks, about how many of them there are on the road and that many of them are just more truck than most people need. "Big truck vs. small economy car never turns out well. If less people drove huge pickups," he said, "there would be less fatalities." He had four more days to live.

Friday-Saturday: January 8-9, 2016
    Olivia (23), our oldest child and only daughter, was due to come home Sunday afternoon. Manfred and our three boys—Hans (20), Josef (18), and Noah (15)—cut and hauled firewood in the woods around the house while I finished working on our tax return and cooking for the potluck fellowship meal on Sunday. I rarely do the taxes this early, but I felt driven to get it done and out of the way. I was also busy preparing for Josef's annual doctor appointment, scheduled for early Monday morning down in Wasilla. Besides all that, we had a business meeting at church to prepare for, so I was rushing around trying to wrap it all up so we could spend a quiet evening together. I felt a sense of urgency, like if I did not get it all done that night, it would not get done at all.
    Late Saturday afternoon, the boys built a fire on the creek ice out behind our house to burn up branches from the trees they felled that day. As I washed the dishes, I watched them from my kitchen window. I saw Hans sitting alone at the edge of the darkness on a small pile of wood near the fire and I hurried with the dishes so I could go sit with him, realizing I might not get another chance to do so before he left us for wherever life would take him. I felt sadness, like he was gone already, and I missed him even while he sat there silhouetted by the fire, just a stone's throw from the house, a young man alone.
    I considered leaving the dishes until later, but this was my last task and then we could all finally relax and spend some time together before our trip the next day. Maybe it was better I did not go out there to sit with him. I like to believe, with so little time left, the Lord perhaps met with Hans there by the fire and spoke something to his heart. My presence might have been an intrusion. Anyway, he soon came to the house and my last chance to sit with him by a fire was lost.

That evening, the last evening I would have with Hans, our last evening with our three boys together, we sat by the woodstove in our cozy little log house. We watched needles fall from the Christmas tree, not imagining Hans had less than forty-eight hours to live. The fire down on the creek ice went out during the night.

Sunday: January 10, 2016
Church in the morning, then a potluck fellowship meal, followed by the annual business meeting. Afterwards, we all walked together to our parked cars. Hans would drive himself and Noah home in his car, and Manfred and myself and Josef would leave right away in our vehicle for Wasilla, a six-hour drive. We stood in the street with the bright winter sunshine reflecting off the snow. Hans and Noah stood facing me as I made a pouty face and told them I wish I could go home with them and take part in whatever fun they had planned. Hans said, "You'll have fun down there. Make sure you take that long hot bath at the hotel." I noticed they wanted to get going. So, as I usually do, I told them to have fun, but not too much fun, and not to make their sister crazy when she got home. "We won't." Smirks all around. That was the last face-to-face conversation I had with Hans.

We all got in our respective vehicles and Hans took off first to go gas up his car. We followed in our pickup and as we passed the gas station, I looked out the window and waved at my handsome sons as they stood by Hans's car. Hans waved back (as he always did). That was the last wave from my boy. He had a little over twenty-four hours left.

Manfred and I and Josef drove to Wasilla, ate two big pizzas there, and then proceeded to the hotel. From our room, we called home to check in, and it was then that I spoke to Hans for the very last time. I asked him what they did after church. "Functional things," he said. "Worked on my car, cleaned my room, checked our snares. You know—functional things. Olivia cooked dinner when she got home, and we watched a Gunsmoke." He asked me if I took my bath yet and admonished me because I had not. "In the morning," I said. "I'm pretty tired." His last words to me were, "Good night". Mine to him, "Sleep tight and all that—don't let anything bite." He sounded pre-occupied, busy, like he was in the middle of something.

The next evening, after the crash, I went to his room and saw it was all in perfect order—definitely not its usual state. Laundry done and put away, shelves organized, no heap on the floor, everything in its place. He left just one pair of dirty socks. I still have them.

Monday: January 11, 2016, The Day of the Crash

Josef's doctor appointment is at 8:00 a.m. At the hotel, I get up early and enjoy a leisurely bath. At the doctor's, I enquire about treatment for Hans's grass allergy. They give me the information; I thank them and tell the receptionist, "I'll tell him his options when I get home." After we finish with the doctor, we spend an hour in the parking lot of a hardware store fixing a gasket on the truck window, then head over to the gun store to shop for a birthday present for Hans. We are not in any hurry.

They are out of .22 ammo at the gun store, so we spend some time looking for something else to give him. We believe we have all the time in the world. Manfred ends up buying Hans an electric boot dryer, and I decide on a sharp-looking brown and black checked Filson shirt. We had not intended spending so much, but we figure since it is his twenty-first birthday, we can splurge a little. We ended up burying him in the Filson shirt.

We fuel up and head north toward home. Halfway there, we stop at a gas station to stretch our legs and spend an unhurried twenty minutes picking out a snack. Looking around the store, I make a mental note to tell Hans to beware of the postcard rack the next time he travels this way. I settle on a small bucket of ice cream and a bag of corn chips. Hans has a little over two hours left on Earth while I am deciding between Rocky Road or plain chocolate.

Back at home, Olivia cooks a big breakfast for herself and the boys. They do not know it, but this is the last meal for the three of them together. Hans drives to the post office in Nenana, then to Fairbanks to pick up a part for Manfred's car. The part had been sitting in town for some time, so Hans decides to go get it that afternoon and do the repair himself the next day. Since there would be no next day for Hans here on Earth, the following week, Manfred completed the job Hans had started for him. It was important to Manfred to finish the job exactly the way Hans planned.

Over the course of that day, the day of the crash, Hans drives at least four times over the spot from which he will leave us for Heaven. It was to that very spot, at the end of our driveway, that Hans would cajole me into taking him as a little boy so he could wait and watch for his daddy to come home.

Weeks after the crash, as Manfred and I walk along the highway retrieving small items of debris from Hans's car, I recall that some years ago, a car fire occurred near that same place on the highway, to which Hans responded with the fire department. I study the edge of the highway where the car fire happened. I look down at the end of our driveway where he stood as a little boy, gesturing to passing truckers to blow their horns. I examine the spray paint on the pavement, which marks the outline of where Hans's wrecked car spun to a stop and try to envision these events as separate occurrences.

In my mind though, I see Hans on one side of the highway, running around aiding a motorist but, turning my head, I see him sitting dead in his car on the other side. I look around for the little boy who is waiting for his daddy, as vehicles whiz by, throwing snow and icy wind into my face. I stand there holding the metal Volvo insignia which I have just picked up from the ditch. None of it seems real.

In Fairbanks, Hans fuels up and then returns home around 4:30 p.m. with the part for his dad's car. Stuffed in his jacket pocket is the gas station receipt stamped with the date and time: 1/11/16, 2:43 p.m. On that bright winter afternoon, while he casually pumps gas, maybe he scrutinizes the small rust patch developing on the driver's door. It does not enter his mind that the very spot of rust he is planning to repair will soon be the point of impact in a fatal car crash. It does not occur to him he has three hours and fifteen minutes to live.

Back at home, he tinkers on the car some. It is not running quite right, so he turns his attention to the spark plugs. He makes his adjustments and then hops on one of the snow machines to make a quick check on his traps while the engine warms up. The car is running with the headlights on when Manfred, Josef, and I turn into our driveway at around 5:30 p.m. I am disappointed to see the cloud of rising exhaust, illuminated by the headlights, because I think perhaps he must go on an emergency call and will not be home with us this evening.

As we drive in toward the house, we meet Hans coming out on the snow machine. He seems to be in a hurry. He puts the machine into reverse and backs up so we can pass. Our headlights shine directly into his face, causing him to avert his eyes. I see him ahead of us and smile because, in his winter hat, he looks like such a little boy. I notice the smooth curve of his face as the light shines on it. It is the last time I will see his living face.

He sits on the machine with clouds of exhaust enveloping him in the cold light of our low-beams and waits for us to pass. My passenger side window is fogged up, so I do not turn my head as we pass him on our right. I want to stop, roll down my window and say hello, but my head does not turn. I want to look at him through the frosty window, but there is no time to scrape it clear. I want to turn to look at him, but I do not. I feel as if I should not.

I do not know why my head will not turn as we follow the curve of the driveway to the left, away from Hans and toward the house. Sitting there in the truck, with eyes that will look only straight ahead, I sense we are turning a corner in life itself. It is just an impression which I cannot fully explain. I perceive the past and the future are meeting right at this moment. Time seems to be slowed.

Maybe time is not as sequential as we think. God sees everything all at once; perhaps the structure that confines time and makes it into something we can understand is loosened sometimes by God's all-powerful hand. Maybe time spills out of its boundaries occasionally. For Hans, there are less than thirty minutes of time left.

Anyway, I assume I will be with him at the house in a few minutes. Manfred parks and walks over to talk to Hans. I feel pulled in that direction, but I do not go. I hear them talking over by Hans's car, but I cannot make out what they say. I gather up the birthday presents we bought for him a few hours ago in Wasilla. I need to hurry inside and get them wrapped without Hans seeing me. I want to give him the Filson shirt a day early because I am sure he will really like it. I think he suspects we will commence birthday festivities right away, and that is probably one reason he is hurrying.

I take the birthday presents straight to our bedroom and partially close the door. I hear Hans enter the house to get something, but I do not come out; I am busy wrapping his birthday presents. He is so close to me and I do not see him, do not speak to him.

Hans goes back outside and shows Manfred and Noah what he has been doing under the hood of his car. He says to Manfred, "See Daddy, I can't make a mistake. I lined out all the spark plugs and numbered them, so I would put them back in the right order." They talk some more, then Hans gets into his car, still wearing his big snow boots and winter gear, and says to Noah, "I'll be right back." Those were his last words.

He drives to the highway, presumably listening to the engine. He travels the last quarter mile of life's road, planned for him by God before the foundation of the world. He drives his car down the dirt driveway where he learned to walk and to run and to ride a bike.

I often wonder what he was thinking, in those last seconds before the crash, as he rolled along through the winter darkness without a clue he was taking his last breaths. I ponder these things now as I drive along this same stretch of dirt road. What was he thinking at this spot here? And here? Fifteen seconds left. Ten. Five. How many heartbeats did he have left? Was he thinking about us who love him? Was he thinking about me?

Shortly after 6:00 p.m., Noah comes into the house to tell us he heard a crash on the highway and people shouting. It is not unusual for us to hear noises from the highway, as there is a rest area a few yards from the end of our driveway. So, we do not get excited about Noah's announcement. It just does not register with any of us.

It is now around 6:30 p.m. and still no Hans. Olivia tries calling his cell phone, but he has it turned off. We do not see that his phone is right there on the shelf behind her. We make a few "Oh, that guy" Hans jokes while Olivia throws on a jacket to go take a look up at the highway. We assume there is some minor situation there, that Hans has probably come up on it after his test drive and is dealing with it until Nenana EMS arrives. We do not have Hans's or Olivia's fire department radio on, and Olivia does not receive a cell phone call asking her to respond. We hear no sirens. We see no lights. It seems to me now that the Lord shielded us, held us back for thirty minutes, the last thirty minutes of our old life.

At this point, the best I can do is piece together what happened next. I did not go to the highway, and so I did not witness all that went on there. There is much I do not know, so I may not have everything right here.

Noah drives Olivia to the highway on the snow machine, drops her off a short distance from the end of the road, and comes back a few minutes later. I put Hans's newly wrapped birthday presents under the nearly dead Christmas tree and sit down in the green wingback chair. Manfred lays down for a quick nap while we wait for Hans and Olivia to get back.

And I begin to think. *It could be Hans. If it is Hans, maybe he is not hurt too badly. He will walk in soon with a few cuts and bruises and say he is alright. Or maybe it is not Hans. Maybe he will need someone to bring his car home because he must drive the ambulance to the hospital.* Noah goes back to the highway to see if he can find out what is going on.

Manfred starts thinking, too. He gets up and walks to the highway to find Hans and Olivia. Now, Noah returns to the house. He has seen the crash scene but, in the darkness and the confusion, has not seen Hans or Olivia.

"Well, it's Hans," he says, "and he's hurt."

I think, *Oh no, his car. He will be very upset about wrecking his car. For two years he has worked so hard restoring it.* Noah looks concerned and very much older than when he left.

I start preparing for a trip to the hospital. I put our healthcare ministry card in my purse and also an extra set of keys to Hans's car in case he has left for the hospital already and has his keys on him. I change my skirt, but I do not put on my winter boots because that would mean I really believe Hans is hurt badly enough to go to the hospital and I do not want to be an alarmist or overreact. But I want to be ready to go, just in case. So, there I sit in the green chair again, waiting for someone to walk back from the highway and tell me what is going on.

And then my eye falls on the December newsletter from Slavic Gospel Association, lying there on the end table, right next to our nativity scene with the figurines still set up: Joseph and Mary and her baby boy. On the cover of the newsletter, I read these words:

"Lord, if you want me to lay my son on the altar, I will."

I go to our bedroom, quietly closing the door behind me. And by the bedside, this bed my husband and I built with our own hands, where Hans's daddy read him stories, the bed underneath which our children made forts and where I now store Hans's things, next to this bed I pray and calmly lay our son on the altar. I do not like doing it. I cannot say my heart is in it. But I do it. I am not a cheerful giver, but neither do I give him up grudgingly. I feel a sense of foreboding, but there is no struggle. I believe this is what I need to do. It is the only thing *to* do. The altar is the safest place for Hans to be.

I am feeling way too calm, dreadfully, horribly calm. I am ready for it. Back to the green chair to wait. I get up and walk to the woodstove and see Manfred and Olivia through the window in our front door, walking to the house. I look at their faces as they reach the door; they look normal, no expression, no hint in their faces. It cannot be too bad. I feel slightly relieved. Manfred comes through the door first. He takes the four steps needed to reach me, clutches me to him while crying out the unbelievable, the irreversible:

"Hans is dead!"

I briefly think he must be mistaken, that he has misunderstood. If Olivia had not been there, I would not have believed him.

A sickening calm comes over me, a profound and terrifying acceptance. I see nothing and no one but Manfred weeping. I am afraid he will die right there in front of me. His pain is shattering. My heart breaks for him. We hold each other, and then I get him to sit down at the kitchen table, reminding him over and over that Hans is with the Lord. He calms down some, but then the next great wave of grief comes, and he just sobs, *"Hans, my Hans! My son!"*

We need help. I need someone to help Manfred. A man. Manfred needs a big, strong man to help him. Pastor Bob—he has lost a child, too—I will call him. I call Pastor Bob at his house. No answer. I call Pastor's family. No answer. I call a church member. Nothing. I call another church member. Pastor Bob is with him, playing dominoes over at the senior center. I say the awful words. He will be right over.

But the highway is closed (for 6 hours) as they work to extricate Hans from the car, do their investigative work, and clear the scene. Olivia goes back to the highway to stay with Hans. When she returns, an Alaska State Trooper comes to take our statements. It is not clear yet exactly what caused the crash or how it happened.

The crash report later showed that Hans pulled out in front of the pickup truck while making a left turn onto the highway from our driveway. We believe his big, size-twelve snow boot may have gotten stuck behind the brake pedal, preventing him from stopping his car in time. Braking with his left foot would have also pushed his right foot down on the accelerator which would explain the spin-marks on the ice right before he entered the highway. Not able to stop, he may have floored it in an attempt to avoid the collision. It is not possible to know for sure what happened.

The pickup truck struck Hans's car in the driver's side door. The damage to the car is astonishing. There is so much traffic backed up, it takes a long time for Pastor Bob to get to us. Then some of our church family comes. They must park at the highway and walk in. And then it seems the entire world is there at our little house.

It is the most trying week of my life—physically exhausting, emotionally grueling. I am thankful for everyone who comes to pay their respects and make sure we eat well. I am thankful for every single gift that is sent to us in the following weeks. I am thankful we were all home together when it happened. I am thankful we returned from our trip a half hour before the crash rather than being stuck in that traffic jam and finding out what happened to Hans while sitting in that long line of vehicles, wondering what the holdup was.

I am thankful. But I am demolished. Stunned and demolished. I am not numb. I am not "In Shock." I have never been more alert in my life. I am feeling it, feeling it *all* while not believing it is possible. And it is huge. Vast. Monolithic. The pain is so fierce it is almost beautiful. I sense it is important to feel it and not to run from it. Anyway, there is no place to run even if I could. We finally go to bed and try to grasp the fact that Hans is not coming home tonight or any night.

But I lie there and watch. I am watching the laminated scripture poster taped to our bedroom door. I referred to this poster often when Hans was a little boy. I am watching this poster because when a car comes down our driveway, the headlights shine through the living room window and onto the glossy laminated surface of the poster, reflecting the light right into my eyes and waking me up. It is very handy for letting me know when our older children get home.

I watch for a very long time—most of the night—and no headlights come. Hans is not coming. But he always comes home; no matter how bad the weather or highway conditions, he always comes home. But not this time. Oh, God. Not this time. Not tonight. Hans is not coming home. Ever.

His bed is empty. My heart is breaking. I do not sleep. I do not think or remember. I just lie there in the pain and wait for the headlights that are not coming.

~~~

Two nights later, I am in bed again, looking out the window and through the trees to the spot where we will bury Hans's body. Hans cleared this place himself last summer with the brush cutter we bought for him and Noah. He cleared it because we planned to bury the ashes of Manfred's father, Hans's grandfather, there.

I was in the first weeks of my pregnancy with Hans when Opa Ernst came for his final visit to Alaska from Germany, and so Hans never met his grandfather face to face. How odd they should die within two years of each other and be buried together in this place. How strange for Hans to tramp all over his own grave site and not know it.

It is very dark out, but I can see the grave site because Manfred and Josef and Noah have built a large fire to melt the frozen ground. They will keep the fire going through the night and into tomorrow. And then the backhoe will come and carve a place into the earth for us to bury our beautiful boy. Our stamhalter. Our Hans.

*stamhalter: son and heir, firstborn male descendant

As if nothing has happened
It is raining, raining
The trees stand there
dripping indifference
As they have for centuries
Watching me and remembering
Sympathetic but
Unhelpful

They've seen this before
A mother
Weeping

Little leaves on the rose bushes
Graduate into adult leaves
That will never rub shoulders
With your passing boyhood
Never

Tiny flowers struggle
To become luscious fruit
Bursting with life
Then drop to the sodden forest floor
Unnoticed

And the birds, the cheery birds
Have no idea
None whatever
That you are gone—always
Gone

KN

2 JOYSORROW

At first, I was shaken, but looking up, I recovered my strength.
GEORGE WHITEFIELD

Forward. That is the direction I need to be moving. Forward is where our son is. Forward is where I will see my Savior, face to face. Moving forward is not the same as moving on. Moving on is putting the past behind you and trying to forget. Moving on is something I will never do.

This book is part of my strategy for moving forward. If I can document the sweetness of the past as well as the pain of the present, perhaps it will become easier to move forward. If I can get it all on paper, then maybe it will not be forgotten. Hans will not be forgotten.

But of course, it is not possible to get it all on paper. Even a "short" life has millions of moments. And there is much I do not wish to share, private blessings that I want to keep all to myself, treasures that are more precious because no one else saw them. Forgive me if I keep these few jewels for myself. Anyway, how do you get a special look or a smell or a voice, or the sound of laughter onto paper? And even if it were possible, most of it would not mean much to anyone else.

As I began writing, it was mostly for my benefit. It kept me from sitting and thinking too much. It helped keep me from the edge of the chasm. Writing helped to make constructive use of my pain, allowing me to deal with it and be distracted from it at the same time.

But, as the razor-wire anguish eased somewhat, it occurred to me that maybe I should share this experience. During the first weeks and months after Hans went home to be with the Lord, I read every book written by a grieving parent I could get my hands on. I needed to hear from someone who had been through child loss, and I am extremely thankful to those parents who put their own pain into words for the rest of us. I pray this book might help someone, too.

I also read all I could find, written by reliable sources, about Heaven. I would alternate reading books about the *sorrow* of losing a child with books about the *joy* of a place too wonderful for us to imagine.

Sorrow and joy. Joy and sorrow. For me, these two concepts are opposite edges of the same knife blade and I find it difficult right now to experience them as separate emotions. I used to think they were on extreme ends of a spectrum, impossible to experience simultaneously. I did not know joy and sorrow could be so tangled up within a hurting heart, each emotion intensifying the other.

But now I know. During especially painful moments, times when just breathing seems too much, joy rises up through the tears, not to displace the sorrow but to engulf and sanctify it. This overwhelming collision of emotions sometimes comes hard and fast, without warning. Other times I can feel it slowly building and I need to find a place to be alone before it erupts. I have given this crashing wave of sweet and joyful pain a name: *Joysorrow.*

Joysorrow is what I feel when I am nearly collapsing with grief and at the very edge of *I Cannot Do This!* Then, at the very peak of my greatest need, the Lord sends the call of a bird, or a shooting star, or the flash of a memory, or a verse of scripture seemingly written just for me. His comfort washes over me even as the choking, heaving sorrow wells up within my chest. And then I am hushed and still before Him. This is *Joysorrow.*

I know there will be joyful moments in our future: weddings, births, holidays, laughter, plus the small, everyday joys infused with sorrow because Hans is not there to share in it with us. There will always be this sorrow. But I know the joy will be there, too. *Joysorrow.*

So, I have learned that joy and sorrow are two sides of the same coin. One of them is meaningless without the other. Joy redeems and transforms my sorrow. Sorrow tempers and matures my joy. Together they are the stuff of which life is made.

3 CALLED

Verily, verily, I say unto you, Except a corn of wheat fall into the ground and die, it abideth alone: but if it die, it bringeth forth much fruit. John 12:24

Look at the seed of any plant: birch, fireweed, dandelion, wheat. The seed in no way resembles the mature plant it will become: a towering redwood has its humble beginning as a sprout on the forest floor; an oak starts out as an acorn; beans for Sunday dinner require you first sacrifice a bean, plant it in the soil, and then wait for the harvest.

But there is a loss involved: you do not get to keep the seed. Once you have your new plant growing, the seed's job is finished. It is used up in the ground as it nourishes the new seedling. Above ground, sunshine and rain take it from there. First, the seed must die; then comes the fruit. Much fruit.

Likewise, Han's body, the one he lived in while he was with us, the one that, like a seed, was laid to rest in the grave, differs from the body he will inhabit at the resurrection (Philippians 3:21; 1 Corinthians 15). Hans's new body will be like the Lord's glorified body. It will not be earthbound; will not be subject to sickness, weakness or sin. It will be perfect, powerful, incorruptible, indestructible.

Our family has planted precious seed. We have sown in tears; God has promised we will reap in joy (Psalm 126:5). It would have been much less painful for us to see Hans bear fruit in some other way. To see him marry, raise children, minister, bless, laugh, bloom. But this is not what God chose to do. He has a different plan, a better plan. Losing Hans hurts, but it makes all the difference knowing God was in complete control the night of the crash and that His plan is being accomplished. It is just astonishing He would move like this in our family, that he would use our Hans in this unexpected way. I never would have imagined it.

> *He that loveth his life shall lose it; and he that hateth his life in this world shall keep it unto life eternal. John 12:25*

Hans's love for life was rich and exuberant. But he was also restless. On the verge of stepping into the responsibilities of manhood, he was at a point in his life where he was asking: *What it is all about? Why do so many people spend so much energy on things that are not important? What is important? What is the point?* He was just beginning to understand the vanity of so much that passes for living. He was beginning to see, with the eyes of a grown man, that the only hope for the world was for the King of Kings to return and that the programs and efforts of men could never fix the world's problems. Hans did not believe he would make a good preacher, but he did say once that he did not see how a man could justify being anything else.

A few days before the crash, Hans spoke about these things. I could see he was unsure of where he fit in the larger scheme of things. I encouraged him to pray the Lord would show him what he was called to do with his life. I know I prayed many times that the Lord would show Hans just the first step on the path He had ordained for him. A few days later, God's plan became clear: Hans was called to die young.

> *If any man serve me, let him follow me; and where I am, there shall also my servant be: if any man serve me, him will my Father honour. John 12:26*

The very first step in God's plan for Hans happened many years earlier when Hans received the Lord Jesus as his Savior. One snowy Christmas Eve, just nineteen days before his fourth birthday, Hans rode along while our church distributed the *Jesus* film house to house. He was saved and sealed for all eternity that night in the back seat of Don Merrill's pickup truck.

Then, apparently, the next thing for Hans was to live a clean life, work hard, bless his family, become a man, to honor his father and mother, to work for two years rebuilding his car, and then, when the last spark plug was adjusted, to get into it, drive to the highway and pull out in front of a pickup truck on the eve of his twenty-first birthday. Saved in a pickup truck; sent to glory by a pickup truck.

In all this, Hans has served the Lord. He has left a good testimony. He has followed Jesus in death unto life eternal. He was and is the Lord's servant and is with Him even now as I write this.

> *Now is my soul troubled; and what shall I say?*
> *Father, save me from this hour: but for this cause*
> *came I unto this hour. Father, glorify thy name.*
> *John 12:27-28*

I do not believe in accidents. God is on His throne every minute, directing in the affairs of men. The crash did not surprise God that terrible night. He has allowed this tremendous loss because it fits precisely with his plan for the universe. God is love and everything He does is in line with His character. He always does what is right. His children are precious to Him. He is not capricious, negligent, or inattentive. If I thought the crash was "just an accident," a freak chance event, I might just lose myself in despair, in the pointlessness of it. It would take an impossible amount of faith for me to believe the crash was an accident. The precision of the timing and logistics does not allow for mere chance. It was unexpected (by us), but it was not accidental. It was the appointed time. It was an act of love and sovereign purpose.

Our God would not allow this terrible pain unless he had a very, very good reason. I trust Him for that. There is nothing else. I trust Him because He is good and because He does what He says He will do. He is real, and He sees our pain. When we see Hans again, we will know what happened that night and we will also know God's purpose. I am content to wait on God for this.

After he left this earth, Hans received honor from men and women who observed his life and took the time to convey their sorrow and admiration for the fine young man Hans had become. Some wept with us, and we are blessed and honored by their tears. This is one way I believe the Father has honored Hans. (v. 26)

And, more importantly, God is honored. In this painful trial, our Father gives us the opportunity to affirm His goodness. Hans's life and death give occasion for the gospel to be presented in ways that would not have been possible if it had not been for that horrible car crash. It impacted more than a few people. We pray for them daily. We trust the Lord for the fruit.

It was not for nothing, this terrible loss. Yes, our souls are troubled—we miss our Hans. It is a profound and heartbreaking loss. And the pain—the pain is unrelenting. But should we have asked the Lord to save us, and Hans, from this? *But for this cause was Hans brought into the world.* The question is not, *why did Hans die?* The question is, *why did Hans live?*

In the eternal decrees of God, one of the chief purposes of Hans's life was to live and die in a particular place, for a specific time, and in a way unique to him, so that a selected group of people would be exposed to the gospel of Christ at just the right moment for them. Every life Hans touched was part of God's plan for him. Is this not so for all of God's chosen servants?

Hans has already, in the short time since his home-going, gotten the good news of Jesus Christ into the hands of many, many people. The seed is planted. He has done what he could. Hans has fulfilled his calling.

I do not believe this was the *only* reason for his existence, but my prayer is that because Hans lived, just one person at his memorial service, just one person who knew him, just one who will read this, will come to know the Lord Jesus as Savior and Friend

But couldn't the Lord have accomplished His purpose in some other way? Well, yes, I suppose so. But why should He? Why should dreadful losses like this happen only to other people, other Christians? Why should we read poignant and uplifting stories about how God used other people's losses for His glory? Shall we reap encouragement only at the expense of others? Should we not suffer as others have, as God's people always have, or are we somehow exempt?

Even if we never see fruit because of what happened to Hans, we want it to be abundantly clear to anyone who questions why God allowed this to happen to our family, that we serve a God who is worthy to be praised, even though He took something precious to us. We follow Him, not because he spares us from heartache (because He has not); nor because of anything He gives us or does for us. We follow Him because He is Almighty God who loves us. He knows what He is doing. We trust Him.

If nothing else is ever accomplished, if there is no apparent good that comes about because Hans died, that is fine. We know the host of Heaven rejoices and God is glorified when we praise him in the midst of devastating loss.

Father, glorify thy name.

What a Gathering
Fanny Crosby & Ira Sankey

1. On that bright and golden morning,
when the Son of Man shall come,
And the radiance of His glory we shall see;
When from ev'ry clime and nation
He shall call His people home,
What a gath'ring of the ransomed that will be!

Refrain
What a gath'ring, what a gath'ring,
What a gath'ring of the ransomed in the summer land of love!
What a gath'ring, what a gath'ring,
Of the ransomed in that happy home above.

2. When the blest, who sleep in Jesus, at His bidding shall arise
From the silence of the grave, and from the sea,
And with bodies all celestial they shall meet Him in the skies,
What a gath'ring and rejoicing there will be! [Refrain]

3. When our eyes behold the city,
with its many mansions bright,
And its river, calm and restful, flowing free;
When the friends that death hath parted
shall in bliss again unite,
What a gath'ring and a greeting there will be! [Refrain]

4. O the King is surely coming, and the time is drawing nigh,
When the blessèd day of promise we shall see;
Then the changing in a moment, in the twinkling of an eye,
And forever in His presence we shall be. [Refrain]

4 THE FACTS

In the early months of grieving for our son, sorrow, longing, and anguish felt like a connection to him, a conduit for all I was feeling, a frantic grasping for nearness. To remember him was to be with him. All my conscious thought focused on getting *to* him—right now. To weep was to hold him close. My baby.

This heavy sorrow is what I *feel*. It is not a reflection of what I, as a Christian, believe. I know where our son is, and I believe what God has told me about our eternal home. Why then do I sorrow?

It is because each crashing wave of grief is my flesh crying out for the son who has been taken from me. It is my soul missing his soul. My flesh missing his flesh. It is in my nature to protect and care for my child, and I cannot. This powerlessness assaults a significant portion of who I am: my *motherness*.

I feel I am trapped in grief. That I cannot cease from longing to see him again. That I can never stop sorrowing. That Sorrow just *is*. It is where I am; it is who I am. But, as natural and unavoidable as these emotions are, they are not grounded in faith, but in the flesh. Grief is a hard place, but I must be careful not to stay here too long, for grieving *excessively* is of no practical help to me. Sorrow cannot bring me nearer to Hans *in fact*.

Grieving is difficult, exhausting work that can become counterproductive if indulged in overmuch. There comes a time when sorrow and anguish are not enough anymore. Not that it wears off, or grieving gets easier. It is just that I have come to an awareness that sorrow is not getting me anywhere.

I see that my tears will not bring Hans back. The churning rawness begins to level off, not because the pain is less, but because I am too weary to cry. The sorrow gets quieter, burrows deeper, becomes part of me rather than something I do battle with. Whereas once I thought my heart would explode with pain, I now feel it threatening to implode, to collapse under the stealthy grip of Sadness.

But then, little by little, I find I can smile occasionally while remembering. Instead of seeing empty spaces everywhere, spaces where Hans should be, I begin to see God's hand. The frantic grasping subsides as I look up in wonder, knowing Hans is *up there*.

Slowly, I realize the Lord has provided a better connection to Hans than sorrow and grief, a connection based on the facts as they *are*—not life as it *was*. I see with the eyes of faith that God has provided *Himself*. And the fires of sorrow burn away the chaff of ease, revealing, as only sorrow can, the nearness of God.

The fact is, Hans is not here with me in my present. He is *with the Lord*. This is not a quaint Christian euphemism for "dead." Hans really is **with the Lord**. We have his broken body here with us, buried in a sweet and sunny patch of ground. And yes, he is part of our past, but only in memory and in the evidence that he left behind of his life. But Hans, the real and living Hans, is presently with the Lord Jesus.

It is true that the day on which I last saw our son is moving farther and farther away from me in time. It feels like we are leaving him behind. But to think like this all the time is to look in the wrong direction. If I turn around, I see I am moving *forward* toward the day when we will be together again. Joyful anticipation of the future must replace the desperate grasping for the past. The time between now and then is getting shorter every minute.

Hans is in my *future*. That is where he is **right now**. *And every day that passes is another day closer to seeing him again.* This is not pie in the sky. This is not my "belief" or my "religion." This is for *real*. These are *facts* based on God's sure word, the Bible.

Our Hans is in Heaven in the actual presence of the Lord God Almighty. And this same God, the Holy Spirit, lives within me. God is near, everywhere I go, as I walk with Him. Therefore, are not Hans and I together in the Lord? Staying close to the Lord, keeping my mind on heavenly, eternal things, abiding in Him, keeps me close to Jesus. And somehow, this keeps me near to Hans as well. Nearer *in fact* than Hans might be even if he were still with us on the earth.

For sons grow up. They move away. They transfer their primary devotion to their own growing families. They may make wise decisions or poor ones. They might become ensnared in sin, apathetic or just busy. The world can be a dangerous place for even the most devoted heart.

But Hans is safe from all that. No one can hurt him. He cannot hurt or deceive himself. He no longer sins. *In fact*, sin cannot touch him at all. He is perfectly pure and holy in a way I can never be while bound in my flesh. Though we will not attain perfect holiness while here on this sin-cursed Earth, God desires us to pursue holiness anyway. And He, by His grace, will enable us to do so, as we seek to do His will and walk in the light of His love. Holiness is a stronger connection to my son than sorrow. And *that* is a fact.

~~~

O child of God, death hath lost its sting, because the devil's power over it is destroyed. It is sweet to die in the Lord: it is a covenant blessing to sleep in Jesus. Death is no longer banishment, it is a return from exile, a going home to the many mansions where the loved ones already dwell. The distance between glorified spirits in heaven and militant saints on earth seems great; but it is not so. We are not far from home—a moment will bring us there. Think not that a long period intervenes between the instant of death and the eternity of glory. When the eyes close on earth they open in heaven. Then, O child of God, what is there for thee to fear in death, seeing that through the death of thy Lord its curse and sting are destroyed? And now it is but a Jacob's ladder whose foot is in the dark grave, but its top reaches to glory everlasting.

C.H. Spurgeon

5 TRAINWRECK

How are you doing?

Why does this question make me panicky? It seems like a simple question to which I ought to be able to give a simple reply. But there is no short answer, no easy multiple choice answer other than "all the above." "How are you doing?" is definitely an essay question.

And I know you do not have time to hear all of it, even if I could come up with the words. Right this very minute, I may breathe normally and have the ability to speak. But an hour from now, or thirty seconds from now, I may be running to find a hiding place before the next torrent of tears breaks again.

Anyway, there are no words, in any language, that can capture what I am experiencing. In some cultures, the women wail when someone dies. But even wailing is inadequate. There are some things that cannot be halved by sharing them. Grief is one of those things.

So, I say something like, "Fine" or "OK." I feel bad when I say this, like I am lying. But it really is no lie. When you have been hit by a dump truck but your injuries are not life threatening and someone asks in the emergency room, "How are you doing?" you can truthfully say, "I am OK." But you have still been hit by a dump truck.

I know your question is probably sincere, but I also know you do not really want to hear the whole unpleasant thing and that you are afraid I might actually tell you. You are nervous about the potential for tears and about how you should respond. You have other things on your mind. You know you cannot help. You are Uncomfortable.

Not only that, you are afraid—afraid of triggering an emotional scene and being helpless to do anything to really help. Afraid I might lose it badly and not stop at your personal comfort level. The whole thing is awkward and uncomfortable, and most people instinctively maneuver to avoid discomfort. I know I do.

I think the art of comforting people is a skill we are losing. We do not get the practice like folks who live in less advantaged cultures. Not long ago, most families suffered child loss, or multiple losses, at least once. But, here and now, the bereaved seem to stick out like a sore thumb, or we feel like we do, and sometimes we disturb the carefree life many people feel they have a right to. A grieving family member can be a real wet blanket at a party.

Sometimes, the silence, avoidance, or discomfort we encounter in social situations is selfishness on the part of the non-bereaved—it takes time and effort to deal lovingly with the grieving. But mostly, it is just ignorance and fear. I know this because I used to be one of the uncomfortable ones.

Even when someone really tries to help us in our grief, it is possible they will say something unhelpful. When I am in the depths of grieving, or just plain sad, it is difficult to explain what I am feeling without saying the wrong thing myself. I know it is very probable I will leave my listening friend with a totally wrong idea of what I am experiencing. Being misunderstood compounds the pain and increases my isolation. And so I keep quiet. Sometimes I wish I could be invisible and not have to take part in the chit-chat that is intended to fill the dead air.

Nevertheless, I struggle with being annoyed with those who say and do nothing, and sorry for those who try but know they are falling short in their efforts. I can see the uneasiness on their face, and I feel bad for them. There is just no person on Earth who can fix this, no matter how badly they want to understand and help me.

So, it's like this. Think of me as recovering from a horrible, traumatic injury for which I had to have emergency surgery, under primitive conditions, without anesthesia. Like an amputation with only a stick clenched in my teeth, like in a war. Under cannon fire with snipers all around and no cover. With a dull knife.

Or you can think of me as having survived a train wreck. You know the kind where the locomotive is steaming down the tracks and the Christmas travelers in the dining car are enjoying a wonderful meal with the family, and all is well at the cramped little table.

And then the music swells and the train approaches a bridge, a very high bridge, and you want to shout, "Stop the train!" But the train keeps going and, half-way across, the bridge begins to collapse. In slow motion. And there is no screaming, just falling. Silent falling. Then the survivors are dragged from the wreck down in the gorge, the black and hungry gorge. And the injuries are horrendous. There are not enough bandages in all the world.

I am injured. I am alive, but I am injured and in a lot of pain. I am walking around wounded, though the wounds are not visible. And it is easy for you to cause me additional pain without even realizing it.

Like when you kiss your little boy at the park, and I see you do it. Or when you stand there behind the cash register at the hardware store, young and strong and smiling and very polite and handsome like my Hans. Or when you do not remember him at all. You have nothing to say about him, no memory of him to share with me so I can know he really existed, and it is not just my imagination I had a son.

I just love to hear his name spoken, to hear things you remember about him. So please be patient with me. I cannot speak my feelings without losing it. My faith is strong, and God is good. But the pain is staggering. Do not ask me about that. Don't ask me how I am doing.

> *Have mercy upon me, O LORD, for I am in trouble:*
> *mine eye is consumed with grief, yea, my soul and*
> *my belly. Psalm 31:9*

Love which has not suffered cannot fully understand another heart's pain.

J. R. MILLER 1896

Why does the sound of the wind break my heart?
It carries away the long-ago laughter
Of yesterday's children
And flings it beyond my reach

The wind runs without a care
Along trails blazed by my mighty hunter
Brushing over the fields of your boyhood
As if your absence does not matter

Yesterday's gentle breeze returns empty-handed
Fierce and without mercy
Its icy sting freezes my silent tears
That shatter upon a future that never was

The wind lies to me
Telling me it goes to where you are
It tosses treetops that sport leaves you never saw
It races through the yard as if you never existed
It blots out the noise of a world
Where you cannot be found
Where my boy once played
And it whispers to me of tomorrows
Without you.

KN

As for man, his days are as grass: as a flower of the field, so he flourisheth. For the wind passeth over it, and it is gone; and the place thereof shall know it no more. Psalm 103:15, 16

6 RACKET

This summer, our first without Hans, has been like no other. Besides Hans being gone, the rest of the family has been away from home for much of the summer work season.
And it is very quiet.
One of the first things that struck me after Hans went to be with Jesus, was how still our house became. Of course, when death comes to a home, a subdued atmosphere is to be expected. But this is a different kind of quiet.
It is like walking deep inside a busy factory, with the clamor of activity all around, when, suddenly, the power is cut, and an abrupt and shocking silence sucks the energy from the room. The very air seems to drop to the floor.
It is like standing near a jetliner, the engines winding to a shriek, as the pilot prepares for takeoff. Then, as the jet disappears into the distance, the silence swirls in and fills the surrounding air. When my ears stop ringing, I hear birds singing in the distance and insects rustling in the brush at my feet, the sounds of life going on around me, without me, and those small noises make the world seem even quieter—close, but far away, like Hans.
Our home now, with half of us gone most of the time, is like a movie with the sound turned off, or a photo album filled with pictures in which there are no people. I go outside and look around the

yard. Where are the people? Where is my family? There were six of us here just a minute ago.

It is hunting season. I listen for shots in the distance that mean someone has taken a moose for the freezer. I remember when Hans got a moose, his first moose, on the first day of the season. He called me on the radio to tell me. It seems so long ago; who were those people? Now I pick up the same radio, but I cannot call him. I can push the button and speak, but he will not answer. He is out of range. There are no shots in the distance at all this year, which is very unusual. Shots in the woods—whether from Hans's big hunting rifle, his .22, or a pellet gun—that is one of the sounds I miss most. The sound of a boy in the woods.

Soon, winter will be upon us and we will burn wood to heat the house and to cook our meals. Hans's chainsaw is sitting in the freezer shed right next to his brother's, right where he left it that Saturday before the crash. Manfred and the three boys had been cutting trees into firewood and stacking it to haul later. Now, our two younger boys will haul that stack without their brother. We will have one less saw running this winter. A chainsaw in the woods—another sound I am missing on this fall day.

And then there is the noise that was Hans himself; the shouting, the laughing, the outrageous sounds he could make; running across the lawn issuing orders, tying a fox pelt or an empty plastic sled behind a goat and enjoying the ensuing chaos; the minor explosives he constructed, and the belly laugh he erupted into after a successful detonation. Hans did not simply enter the house. He hurtled into it and then filled it. When he was younger, I had to remind him that the house was small and that he must not use up more than his share of the available air space. We have airspace to spare, now.

So, these days I sometimes sit and listen to the quiet and remember the sounds of the past. I listen carefully for a noise that might be Hans. I hear only the chickadees and the squirrels and my own heart which, incredibly, keeps beating.

I am standing upon the seashore. A ship at my side spreads her white sails to the morning breeze and starts for the blue ocean. She is an object of beauty and strength. I stand and watch her until, at length, she hangs like a speck of white cloud just where the sea and sky come to mingle with each other. Then someone at my side says: "There, she is gone!"

"Gone where?"

Gone from my sight. That is all. She is just as large in mast and hull and spar as she was when she left my side and she is just as able to bear her load of living freight to her destined port. Her diminished size is in me, not in her. And, just at the moment when someone at my side says: "There, she is gone!" there are other eyes watching her coming, and other voices ready to take up the glad shout: "Here she comes!"

And that is dying.

HENRY VAN DYKE

7 OLD YELLER TRUCK

The other day I went to the yellow pickup to see if Hans left anything in there. Sure enough, there was his Forestry Department issued clothing from when he worked for them his last summer, helping for a few days on a wildfire south of Nenana. It was all folded up neat as a pin and piled on top of the emergency crash bag he and his sister kept in the truck.

Because they were first responders, the crash bag always stayed in the truck. And because it cold-started reliably in sub-zero temperatures, the old yellow pickup truck was their vehicle of choice when responding to emergency calls. You do not want to cold-start your primary vehicle at those temperatures if you can avoid it.

He had folded the yellow shirt and the green pants from Forestry very precisely, leaving the red bandana on top, still twisted like he had just taken it off. On top of that were his goggles and yellow hard hat. His heavy lace-up boots were there, too. The clothes were smudged with soot and the boots were caked with mud. He must have expected to go back to the fire, or he would not have left his boots with mud on them; he was very particular about his footwear. But maybe it rained or something, or the fires burned themselves out, and then he got busy and forgot about the clothes and boots in the yellow pickup truck.

Four and a half months later, the yellow shirt still smells strongly of summer smoke. I brush the caked mud off a boot and think about bringing all of it into the house and throwing it on the floor of his room in a heap like he did when he came home tired.

And pretend he is still here.

Everything is necessary, which God sends. Nothing is necessary, which God withholds. How happy are those who can resign all to Him, who see His hand in every trying dispensation, and who believe that He chooses better for them than they could possibly choose for themselves! Faithful are the wounds of that Friend who was Himself wounded and slain for us, and who now reigns over all!

Christ is sovereign over all of our trials. He is the Supreme Disposer of all that concerns us, that He numbers the very hairs of our heads, appoints every trial we meet with—in number, weight, and measure, and will allow nothing to befall us, but what shall contribute to our good. The view of trials as a necessary medicine suited to our disease, powerfully reconciles us unto every cross.

What a comfort to be assured that our afflictions do not happen to us at random—but are all under the direction of infinite wisdom and love, and all engaged to work together for good to those who love the Lord!

JOHN NEWTON

8 TENACIOUS

Several years ago, high winds snapped a large spruce tree about halfway up its trunk, sending the upper part of the tree crashing down onto the roof of our house as we slept. Damage was minimal, the roof was repaired, and the tree was cut up and hauled away for firewood. But the stump, about eight feet tall, remained.

Hans cut the top off the jagged, lifeless pillar about five feet from the ground and then used his router on the flattened surface to create a bird feeder. We enjoyed watching many kinds of birds from our bedroom and living room windows.

Sometime later, I placed a flowerpot on top and used the stump as a planter. I liked seeing petunias cascading over the edge of the pot and down the rough bark. But eventually, the stump became infested with carpenter ants and, since the twelve-inch diameter stump was only a few feet from our house, the ants sometimes visited the neighbors—us. So, Hans decided the stump had to go.

I disagreed. I enjoyed the stump and the fact that since it was right outside our bedroom window, I could lay right in bed and enjoy my petunias or the occasional woodpecker looking to snack on an ant. We went back and forth on it for a time; me wanting to keep the stump and him wanting to remove it.

I *liked* the stump. Maybe I wanted to keep it because, when Hans was about eight years old and the stump was still a healthy, fifty-foot tree, I shot a squirrel out of the top of it with one shot from Hans's .22 rifle. He and his sister were not just impressed, they were astonished. A mommy who can shoot?! It was the shot heard round the house for many years to come. I scored big points that day in the eyes of my little boy.

But, alas, finding no support from any quarter, I gave in. The stump was an eyesore and a carpenter ant factory. I would miss it, but the stump would have to go.

So, last summer—Hans's last summer with us—he cut it flush with the ground with his chainsaw. Then he dug and dug and pulled and pushed. He sawed and chopped and sweated and regretted. It was hot, dusty, frustrating work.

It took many weeks of toil on his days off from work. I just could not understand why, after working so hard all week, he would punish himself with this stump. But he was determined. The stump was an enemy he must vanquish, conquer, annihilate. And all the ants, too. It was war. He would not give up. Ever.

He informed me that the wild rose bush which had grown near the stump would have to go, too. The roots of the stump passed right through where the rose bush grew. Collateral damage. I knew it would be useless to argue. He dug up the lush and beautiful rose bush and we stuck it in a barrel of water.

Finally, all the roots of the stump were out, leaving a crater about five feet across and two feet deep. Hans filled in the crater, carefully smoothed it over, planted grass seed, and covered the area with straw. He tried to talk me into ditching the now extremely sorry looking rosebush and replacing it with a nice store-bought rose bush.

No, I liked that one.

So, he replanted it for me. But it was not looking well, and we were all certain it would die before the end of summer. No way could it survive the winter after what it had been through. But the rose bush held on, just a bunch of thorny sticks with a few yellow leaves. The grass seed sprouted into a tidy patch of grass; the rose bush limped along through the rest of summer, fall, and then winter.

Then January. And a car crash. And our Hans was gone.

As I lay in bed now and look out our bedroom window, I have an unobstructed view through the space where the stump used to stand, where the petunia flourished, and the woodpecker visited. I can see all the way across the yard, through the trees to where Hans and his grandfather are buried. And, like the rosebush, I wonder how I will survive the winter.

Time passes. I look out and see the gravesite and it occurs to me that if the stump were still there, it would block my view of the cross we planted there five months ago. Looking from the pillow where I rest my head during the darkless Alaska summer night, in a straight line to the spot where Hans's body now rests, I realize the old stump would be directly in my line of sight.

Why was he so driven to remove that stump? At the time, I thought he was a tad obsessed with it.

But now I see.

And this spring, the rose bush bloomed.

9 LIGHT SHOW

Hans was a flashlight fanatic. This, of course, led to a rechargeable battery habit. He did not want to get caught on a highway emergency call without a good light; and car repairs and other chores at home often had to be done during the dark days of winter, making a high quality, fully charged light indispensable. An exceptional flashlight or headlamp is considered a status symbol in some circles. And considering how much we depend on our lights, rechargeable batteries make the whole flashlight thing more economical.

So, not unexpectedly, Hans's last Christmas gift to his dad was a battery charger, über alles, to replace our old smaller one. They both had been eyeing this gadget for some time, so it is surprising they did not end up giving each other the same gift. Manfred was thrilled, and Hans was pleased that his dad was thrilled. They immediately began charging batteries with abandon.

A few years before Hans left us, Manfred splurged on a slick LED flashlight for Hans's birthday. It is heavy, but not too large, and has a zoom feature that allows you to widen the stream of light or to draw it down to a tightly focused square-shaped beam. This baby throws enough lumens to light up a mountainside. OK, so maybe not a whole mountainside, but a good-sized hillside for sure.

Like the one above the bank of the Tanana River, across from the town of Nenana, Alaska. It was the annual winter fireworks spectacular and, being a member of the Nenana Volunteer Fire Department, Hans got to take part in putting on the pyrotechnic show for the town. This, of course, was right up Hans's alley.

The Fire Department folks set up across the frozen river and began launching fireworks, showers of sparkling color cascading nicely over the ice. An impressive *boom* followed each dazzling explosion. From where we sat on the opposite bank, the snow-covered hillside bordering the river provided the perfect backdrop. It was all sparkling bursts of color against the black sky, the glowing snowy night awash with color after each successful launch. It was magnificent. But this mother's eye was drawn to something else.

Bouncing around at the base of the hill, across the river that lay frozen between the fireworks techs and us spectators on the dock, was a light. A flashlight. A very bright flashlight. I saw the stream of light widen and play upon the hillside. Then the beam narrowed into a tightly focused square-shaped beam. I saw the beam swing in my direction, then away again, then continue its cavorting as I watched. The beam of light again shone in my direction, then blinked on and off a few times. Then the strobe feature activated. It was an unmistakable signal from my flashlight fanatic son who was not about to be upstaged by any fireworks extravaganza. That night, in plain view of the entire town, I was treated to a private light show. Just for me.

Fast forward to last night. To a mother shivering outside under the October sky, eyes peering into the blackness, straining to see into the deep far away where she knows her son lives. She tries desperately to see beyond the stars to where he is. She gazes across the river of time and space and knows she cannot cross and neither can her son. Not yet.

She whispers his name as if he were near, then says it louder. She shouts his name. And at that precise moment, right when his name bursts from her heart, a shooting star streaks across the sky.

Just for her.

Afflictions cannot injure when blended with submission. Ice breaks many a branch, and so I see a great many persons bowed down and crushed by their afflictions. But now and then I meet one that sings in affliction, and then I thank God for my own sake as well as his. There is no such sweet singing as a song in the night.

You recollect the story of the woman who, when her only child died, in rapture looking up, as with the face of an angel, said, "I give you joy, my darling." That single sentence has gone with me years and years down through my life, quickening and comforting me.

Henry Ward Beecher

10 FOUR

It is a Sunday afternoon in summer. Our first summer without Hans. Manfred and Noah are three hundred miles away on a job in Anchorage. Olivia, Josef and I are back home after church and have eaten our spaghetti, with ice cream for dessert. Olivia leaves for work and Josef hops on his bike. I clear the table and head outside.

It is an astonishingly beautiful day. Which makes it worse. Sundays can be especially tough for me. I miss having everyone at home all together.

I take a turn around the garden. I often go to there to think and to remember. I pause at the far end, beyond the cabbages and the potatoes, out in the little meadow, and look back at the house, our sweet little house all covered with flowers and filled with memories.

The sun casts cool shadows on the freshly mown lawn as I drift back into the not so very long ago. In my mind and heart, I see our four children rolling around on the grass with a couple of goat kids, a puppy, a bunny or two. They are loafing and laughing and just messing around and being together. I have spent some of the best moments of my life secretly watching the four of them play together on that lawn.

It is not just Hans I miss. It is all of them together as happy, playful children on an ordinary Sunday afternoon. Sometimes I so want to turn back the clock to one of those precious days. Or to turn it forward to when we will all be together again. But I cannot. And I miss them so very much.

So, I am out there alone in the little meadow beyond the garden, crying of course—crying hard. I look over at the house again, then at the workshop and the animal pens. *Where are my children?* I listen for shouts and laughter but I hear nothing. Nothing but a little sparrow whose call says *Mommy I'm OH-ver here*. I look up. Up is the best place to look. Up is where Hans is.

And then I see them. Three young eagles circling high overhead. They gain altitude on the rising summer heat without ever flapping a wing. I see a fourth eagle. It zooms at the other three and then zooms away again in a provoking sort of way, like Hans used to do when he was being rascally. It seems to keep apart from the others, but not too far away. Rather like how it is now, with Hans. Here, but not here.

Then, a short time later, or maybe it was a long time, the fourth young eagle rejoins the others as they play eagle games, soaring for the joy of it, just messing around and being together on a Sunday afternoon in summer. Four of them. Together.

And from a secret place, the mother eagle watches.

11 COMPELLED

It is over seven months now since Hans left us for Heaven, yet I still get these illogical, unrealistic compulsions to find him. For instance:

It is a beautiful breezy day; it is hot, and the birds are singing: *He must be out in the woods or hiking along the railroad tracks. If I start walking now, I will come across him on the trail. He is out there somewhere. Maybe he is napping in the sun. Maybe he is hurt and is waiting for somebody to come help him. Maybe he has been out there alone all this time, wondering why no one has come.*

Or I hear traffic on the highway: *He must have gone off somewhere in his car. Maybe he went to Canada after all. Maybe he will be back soon. If I get in our car right now and start driving, I will eventually come to the place where he is. I do not care how far it is or what it costs to get there, I just have to get to where he is.*

Or it is the middle of the night, very dark up on his empty bed, and I look at the black and vacant space where he slept all his life, and then out the window to where his car should be parked. But nothing is there but cold moonlight. I walk from room to room, but I cannot find him. *He must be out on an ambulance call. He will be home soon. I will sit here and wait, and he will come home as he always has. I will see his headlights any minute. If we still had his radio, I could listen to the traffic and know when the ambulance is back in quarters, and then he will be home not longer than a half hour after that because it is late, and they will just clean the ambulance tomorrow.*

He is out there. I must find him...

12 NEW FRIENDS

In these past nine months since Hans drove to the highway, I have dreamed of him only once. It occurred shortly after he left us, and it was very brief.

In my dream, Sunday worship had just concluded, and Hans was standing with a group of men outside on the lawn in front of the church. I did not recognize any of the men. I could tell they were all engaged in a conversation of some depth and import. Our youngest son, Noah, was there in the group, too, at the edge, observing and listening, but not really a part of the conversation.

Hans turned to look at me. His expression said, "Don't worry, I'm fine. I can't go home with you. This is important." He smiled a happy and reassuring smile, waved, and then turned back to the conversation. He had no desire to leave this group of men, and I sensed he knew I understood he was exactly where he was supposed to be; that it was necessary for him to remain. He was not hungry and wanting to get home to spaghetti dinner. He was not interested in anything but what was being discussed in this group of men. He was totally calm and serious, clearly comfortable with these men and very involved in what was being said. Noah then walked away from the group of men to where I was standing.

End of dream.

13 WELL SAID

Though written by me in the voice of our son Josef, (who has Down syndrome), the following piece was intended as a thank-you from myself to Hans for all his help in caring for his younger brother. Each member of our family contributes to meeting Josef's needs, and I wanted to thank Hans, in writing, for doing his part. He never expected a thank-you, which is why I so wanted to give him this one. I planned on giving this to Hans on his twenty-first birthday. Even though I was not able to, I trust he was told about it and is very much pleased with his final reward.

~~~

Sometimes, when I am thinking about something that makes me feel mad or sad, I can't put enough words together to explain how I feel. Sometimes, I just need to say something, and I don't know how to say it, or I can't say it fast enough and everybody just keeps talking without me. But you would always stop and wait and ask me what I wanted to say and then make me say it.

Lots of times, it's just too much trouble to say something clearly, like "church" or "spaghetti". But you would show me with your mouth how to say it over and over until I got it almost right. And when I got mad because I couldn't talk like everyone else, you would tell me to "quit it" in your almost Daddy voice. That made me even madder; but it worked. Then, I could be happy again. Sometimes, when you were making me do things for myself, Mommy would tell you to back off and don't push me so hard. But I think it was good that you did that. I still don't like saying "Good morning" at the breakfast table, but you would always keep after me until I said it. I didn't like that, but I said it, so I could finally eat my oatmeal.

The other day I was trying to nail up a board onto Noah's tree fort. I just couldn't do it. Mommy wanted to help me, but I wanted to do it myself, like you. Your grave marker is not far from the tree fort, and I think Mommy was sad because you were not there to help me. She kept looking at the spot where you are buried and then at me, and then she went back to the house.

I still can't tie my shoes or cut my meat. You were working on the shoe tying thing with me just before you left us. And when my bicycle chain falls off, I can't fix it by myself yet. I found the right socket wrench in your toolbox, but I couldn't turn the bolt. Sometimes someone will do something nice for me and I'll forget to say thank you. Noah and Livvy help me and remind me now, but they're not always here, so Daddy or Mommy does it.

Back when I wasn't doing too good and I couldn't talk, and I wasn't very much fun, you never gave up on me. You liked to teach me things and you would show me one step at a time that I could do it. I never got a chance to say thank you. I will be nineteen next week Hans. A big man like you. If I could talk as good as you, I would say thank you for being my friend and my brother. And I would try to say it very good.

I can't wait until you come back with Jesus.

graveside 1/16/16

14 WHAT HANS BELIEVED

Experiencing the wrenching pain of child loss has helped me to recognize more fully that most grieving people have an intense need for hope and assurance they will someday be reunited with their loved ones. Assurance and hope based on facts leads to peace and can take the edge off grief when it threatens to escalate to despair.

False hope, however, which is a counterfeit assurance based on error, can make one *feel better*, but only temporarily. In the still small hours of a sleepless night, one needs something more substantial than "I hope to see him again." By now, if you have read this far, it is apparent that I am quite certain of seeing Hans again. Heaven is a real place. My son is there. I am sure of this as a person can be.

I have observed people who do not believe in an afterlife; the anger, guilt and despair they often carry on top of their grief can be shattering. Likewise, the mourner that senses there must be something more to our brief existence on the earth, but has no concrete ideas about it, is vulnerable to being lost in a quagmire of error that may bring temporary relief, but not true and lasting peace.

There are various pleasant-sounding popular notions about death and dying to choose from that seemingly help make the pain more bearable. Here are a few I have run into:

Everybody goes to Heaven, *no questions asked.* This does not bring peace because it violates one's innate sense of justice. Under this system, the murderer and the victim both go to Heaven. No sin occurred; no penalty is paid. Mercy is granted to all because all are essentially good somewhere deep inside. In addition to straying far from the facts, this arrangement stands justice on its head, satisfying no one. I believe, deep down, most people that hold this view know it cannot work this way.

> *And these shall go away into everlasting punishment: but the righteous into life eternal.*
> *Matthew 25:46*

My child is not gone. *He is right here with me; I just cannot see him.* Comforting as this thought is, I believe most parents, if they are honest, suspect it is not true. It is a little lie we tell ourselves when the longing for our child becomes overwhelming. We confuse past memories with present desire, combining them within our imagination in a desperate attempt to make it so. Comforting? Maybe for a time. But it is a fragile self-deception that can compound the pain.

It is tempting to think, since God is omnipresent, and Hans is with Him, that maybe Hans is omnipresent, too—that my son is with me wherever I go. But this is a not an idea at all supported by scripture. Only God is omnipresent. God's word says that when Jesus returns,

> *them also which sleep in Jesus will God bring with him. 1Thessalonians 4:14*

God will not bring with Him someone who is already here. No, Hans is gone—gone to Heaven to be with the Lord. He is done with this old groaning world.

There is no Heaven, *there is only energy, and when I leave this planet, I will join all the other energies out there, one of which is my child, and we will co-exist forever in a state of blissful harmony.* This is fantasy with no basis in fact. One might make this sound quasi-scientific but trying to prove this nonsense would be an impossibility. Assurance? Hardly. Heaven is an actual place; how much better is sure hope from God's word:

> *But lay up for yourselves treasures in heaven, where neither moth nor rust doth corrupt, and*

> *where thieves do not break through nor steal:*
> *Matthew 6:20*

This is all there is. There is no afterlife. I have nothing to look forward to except death, which will finally end my pain. No hope with this view. But look what is in store for those who believe:

> *And God shall wipe away all tears from their eyes;*
> *and there shall be no more death, neither sorrow,*
> *nor crying, neither shall there be any more pain: for*
> *the former things are passed away. Revelation 21:4*

I understand how easy it is to grasp at anything plausible that offers assurance that we will see our children again, that they are not really gone, or that it does not even matter. But plausible is not good enough. I want the Truth. I want reality. I want what actually *is*. Anything else will not help me and certainly will not do Hans any good. I have the Truth. I do not need fairy tales.

So, how can I be so confident that I will see my son again? Is it because he was "a good boy," was "never in any trouble," "was no worse than anyone else?" Is it because his family goes to church every Sunday and Hans never missed a meeting unless he was sick? Is it because his parents are Christians? No, no and no.

> *Not by works of righteousness which we have done,*
> *but according to his mercy he saved us*
> *Titus 3:5*

There is only one assurance I can claim concerning where Hans is today. That assurance lies in the person and work of Jesus Christ and in the promises He has given us in His Word:

> *Jesus said unto her, I am the resurrection, and the*
> *life: he that believeth in me, though he were dead,*
> *yet shall he live: And whosoever liveth and be-*
> *lieveth in me shall never die. Believest thou this?*
> *John 11:25-26*

So here it is in a nutshell: Hans, like all of us, like me, and like you if you are honest, was a sinner by nature, by birth, by choice and by practice. Hans knew this.

> *For all have sinned, and come short of*
> *the glory of God; Romans 3:23*

> *If we say that we have no sin, we deceive ourselves,*
> *and the truth is not in us. 1 John 1:8*

Hans knew he could not get rid of this sin problem by himself. He knew he needed a Redeemer and Savior, Someone to take his penalty for sin and to satisfy God the Father's holy justice. No one gets away with anything—Hans knew this, too.

> *For the wages of sin is death; but the gift of God is*
> *eternal life through Jesus Christ our Lord.*
> *Romans 6:23*

Jesus is God the Son, which makes Him the only qualified Person to act as our substitute and to take the punishment we deserve. There is one way into God's Heaven. Jesus is it. Hans knew this as well.

> *Jesus saith unto him, I am the way, the truth, and*
> *the life: no man cometh unto the Father, but by me.*
> *John 14:6*

> *For there is one God, and one mediator between*
> *God and men, the man Christ Jesus; 1 Timothy 2:5*

> *Neither is there salvation in any other: for there is*
> *none other name under heaven given among men,*
> *whereby we must be saved. Acts 4:12*

So far, so good. But what did Hans do with all this? He believed it. That's it. That is why I am so sure I will see Hans again. Because I believe what Hans believed. What keeps you from believing, too?

What Hans Believed

For God so loved the world, that He gave His only begotten Son, that whosoever believeth in Him should not perish, but have everlasting life. John 3:16

For I delivered unto you first of all that which I also received, how that Christ died for our sins according to the Scriptures; And that He was buried, and that He rose again the third day according to the Scriptures: 1 Cor 15:3-4

For by grace are ye saved through faith; and that not of yourselves: it is the gift of God: Not of works, lest any man should boast. Ephesians 2:8-9

Verily, verily, I say unto you, He that heareth My word, and believeth on Him that sent Me, hath everlasting life, and shall not come into condemnation; but is passed from death unto life. John 5:24

15 TRUSTING GOD WITH YOUR CHILD'S ETERNITY

*Trust in the LORD with all thine heart; and lean not
unto thine own understanding.*
Proverbs 3:5

Our son, Hans, had his faults. Like you and like me, he was a sinner. However, Hans *was saved*—he was a Christian—one who has placed his trust in Jesus Christ alone for salvation. When just a small boy, God saved Hans from the penalty and power of sin, assuring him a place in Heaven based on faith in Jesus' death, burial, and resurrection. So, when we say we will see Hans again, our level of assurance is quite high.

But what about the parent who does not have that assurance? What about the parent who is not sure *at all*? Perhaps you are thinking: *What if all this stuff about Heaven and Hell is true? I have no reason to believe my child knew anything about Jesus. What if I failed to tell my child the most important thing in all the world? What if my child is now eternally lost? How can I ever live with such a possibility? How could Heaven be bliss for me without my child?* **How could God let this happen?**

Here is what you must hold on to: God is good. God is love. God makes no mistakes. If we do not believe these facts about God, we are sunk. The pain is just too much to bear unless we trust the Lord God Almighty. Here are a few more facts:

God loves children. Pre-born people, people born with limited mental capacity, infants, and young children who are not yet of sufficient age as to be held accountable for their actions are *safe*. When they die, they go to be with the Lord in Heaven.

> *And they brought young children to him, that he should touch them: and his disciples rebuked those that brought them. But when Jesus saw it, he was much displeased, and said unto them, Suffer the little children to come unto me, and forbid them not: for of such is the kingdom of God. Verily I say unto you, Whosoever shall not receive the kingdom of God as a little child, he shall not enter therein. And he took them up in his arms, put his hands upon them, and blessed them.*
> *Mark 10:13-16*

> *But now he [King David's infant son] is dead, wherefore should I fast? can I bring him back again? I shall go to him, but he shall not return to me. 2 Samuel 12:23*

What about those who trusted Christ as children but then go on to live a wayward life? This is more difficult. However, if they were truly born again, they are eternally secure in their salvation, and nothing can snatch them from the Father's hand. Nothing.

However, it also possible the child's profession of faith was not authentic. If that is indeed the case, the best and only recourse is to trust God for whatever outcome He has ordained, accepting by faith that, when we see Christ face to face, we will be in full accord with His perfect will. Oh, how hard this is! To a grieving parent, this does not set well *at all*. Everything in us screams *NO!* to such a possibility.

We cannot alter the past, but if there is a shred of realistic hope the child was genuinely born again, hang on to that. Discipline your mind and resist the temptation to imagine what you cannot know for sure. Do not torture yourself. Focus on your loved ones who remain, the ones you can still actually help. And if your child *is* in Heaven, be sure you will be there, too.

God always does right. God is good. We must trust Him. We must leave it all with the Lord and ask Him to grant us peace.

God is merciful. The thief who was crucified on a cross beside the Lord, believed Jesus was Who He said He was—King of Kings and Lord of Lords. The thief knew he was a sinner deserving death and called Jesus *Lord*. No special prayer, no good works, not much time to do anything other than believe.

> *And one of the malefactors which were hanged railed on him, saying, If thou be Christ, save thyself and us. But the other answering rebuked him, saying, Dost not thou fear God, seeing thou art in the same condemnation? And we indeed justly; for we receive the due reward of our deeds: but this man hath done nothing amiss. And he said unto Jesus, Lord, remember me when thou comest into thy kingdom. And Jesus said unto him, Verily I say unto thee, To day shalt thou be with me in paradise.*
> *Luke 23:39-43*

The worst sinner in the world can, while taking his last breath, cry out to God from his heart for mercy. Unless you were with your child one hundred percent of the time throughout his entire life, you cannot know if he may have heard the good news of salvation in Jesus. Unbeknownst to you, your child could have heard about Jesus from a tract, a radio broadcast, a Facebook post, a Bible verse scrawled on a wall, a sign held up at a football game, or a billboard. God does not take pleasure in sending people to Hell.

> *As I live, saith the Lord GOD, I have no pleasure in the death of the wicked; but that the wicked turn from his way and live: Ezekiel 33:11*

God is just. Our children are in the hands of a *righteous* judge. If we know Jesus as our Lord and Savior, we will rejoice in whatever we find when we finally enter eternity. We will see things with God's eyes. We will understand His purposes. We will be in perfect agreement with his sovereign will. There will be no sorrow, no tears, no grieving. We will say, *yes, Lord, I see it now.* We will praise Him for His wisdom and lovingkindness. We will have peace.

> *Gracious is the LORD, and righteous; yea, our God is merciful. Psalm 116:*

> *But let him that glorieth glory in this, that he understandeth and knoweth me, that I am the LORD which exercise lovingkindness, judgment, and righteousness, in the earth: for in these things I delight, saith the LORD. Jeremiah 9:24*

So, while I am quite certain I will see Hans again, I can only be certain up to a point. I cannot see into Hans's heart the way God can. I cannot *know*, beyond any doubt, his profession of faith was authentic. I can look at Hans's life, I can remember his words and what he told us he believed, but I can only be one hundred percent certain of my *own* salvation.

Likewise, you cannot be one hundred percent certain that your child is eternally lost. Not knowing for sure, you will suffer. But there is hope. And there is God. The God you can trust. Even with this.

Yet there is a way of remembering sorrow, which brings no blessing, no enrichment which does not soften the heart, nor add beauty to the life. There is an unsubmissive remembering which brings no joy, which keeps the heart bitter, which shuts out the sunshine, which broods over losses and trials. Only evil can result from such memory of grief.

By standing and weeping over the grave where it is buried, we cannot get back what we have lost. When David's child was dead, he dried his tears and went at once to God's house and worshiped, saying, "Now he is dead, why should I fast? Can I bring him back again?" Instead of weeping over the grave where his dead was not, he turned all the pressure of his grief into the channels of holy living. That is the way every believer in Christ should treat his sorrows.

J.R. Miller (1840-1912)

16 THE BUTTERFLY

Of the many beautiful flowers that were given for Hans's memorial service, only one is still alive and thriving in our home, an orchid, with its one big showy cluster of purple flowers at the end of a long vine-like stem. After we brought it home from the service, wrapped in plastic to protect it from the January cold, it suffered total neglect for several months, losing its flowers and gathering dust. I thought for sure it was unsavable.

But it turns out, an orchid is rather forgiving. I trimmed the yellowed, waxy leaves and gave it a shot of water every week or so. After some months now, it is sporting a new set of leaves and a very grand new cluster of flowers. This exotic bit of tropical rain forest provides a gaudy contrast to the first snow that is falling quietly on the other side of my window.

Around the time of freeze-up, when the summer birds have long deserted us for the south and the leaves have shamelessly abandoned the trees, it is not unusual to find a stray butterfly that has sneaked into the house to avoid the cold. Because they are just butterflies, they do not know they come into the house to die. If it is still warm enough during the day for them to survive, I will catch them and release them back outside. However, if it is just too cold for butterflies anymore, I will let them remain indoors to spend their last days pouting on our windowsill.

I should say here that I do not believe that a butterfly encounter is a sign or visit from my son. God controls the creatures in His creation. He can choose to send me a butterfly as a token of His presence and care, or He may send some other form of comfort. In Alaska, butterflies are not very reliable for comfort or anything else, especially in winter.

Anyway, this year, since I had the orchid in full bloom, I thought I would give this last summer butterfly a real treat. I splashed some water onto the exposed roots and leaves of the orchid so the butterfly could have some moisture. I carefully picked up the sluggish insect, rather brown and dowdy really, for a butterfly, and placed it gently into the little paradise I had arranged for it. It promptly flew back to the windowsill, preferring the cold and dreary view out the window to the lush tropical resort I had provided indoors.

I tried again, this time setting it right in the center of a moist, luscious, fully opened flower. Here was everything a butterfly could desire at the end of October in Interior Alaska. But she would have none of it. This time, she flew to the window frame, dug her little heals into the wood and set her face to the wall.

I check on her every few hours. There she sits, just inches from fresh water and sweet nectar from a gorgeous flower, yet she refuses to partake. She prefers hugging the wall or peering at the cold yesterdays which hide under the snow outside the window. Anything but the joy of the flower.

Maybe she is remembering and longing for the bright summers which are behind her, to which she cannot return. She, being a doomed butterfly, cannot anticipate the joys of the future. She cannot foresee the continuation of life beyond the windowsill. This leaves her in a diminished present that is lifeless and joyless.

Poor, silly butterfly that does not smile. Why must you be so foolish?

Canst thou answer this, believer? Canst thou find any reason why thou art so often mourning instead of rejoicing? Why yield to gloomy anticipations? Who told thee that the night would never end in day? Who told thee that the winter of thy discontent would proceed from frost to frost, from snow, and ice, and hail, to deeper snow, and yet more heavy tempest of despair? Knowest thou not that day follows night, that flood comes after ebb, that spring and summer succeed winter?

Hope thou then! Hope thou ever! For God fails thee not. Dost thou not know that thy God loves thee in the midst of all this? Mountains, when in darkness hidden, are as real as in day, and God's love is as true to thee now as it was in thy brightest moments.

Come, sing in the midst of tribulation. Rejoice even while passing through the furnace. Make the wilderness to blossom like the rose! Cause the desert to ring with thine exulting joys, for these light afflictions will soon be over, and then "forever with the Lord," thy bliss shall never wane.

C. H. Spurgeon

17 BETTER THAN A HIGH FIVE

Don't cry because it's over. Smile because it happened.

Dr. Seuss

Hans always made a point of thanking me whenever I helped him out with something. I believe he thanked me after almost every meal I ever cooked for him. Every pizza was "the best pizza ever."

Often, after asking me to assist him in some way, he would say, "I hope this doesn't cause you more work." And when I did something just for him that he found particularly helpful or amazing, he would express his delight by declaring emphatically, *"You da **Mommy**!"*

For instance, he might ask me to sew a patch on his EMS uniform while I was in the middle of canning carrots: *I hope this doesn't cause you more work.* Of course, he knew it did and he truly didn't want to be a bother, but saying it made him feel better.

So, I would just smile at him and say something like, "Sure, what else have I got to do?" Then he would grin back at me with mischief in his eyes and thank me profusely.

I didn't want him to think I was too busy for him, that he was bothering me. He was always so genuinely appreciative.

Hans would be very dismayed to see the extra work he has caused me recently, this work of grieving. So, I try not to lose myself in the sadness.

And I can't wait to hear him say those words again:

"*You da **Mommy**!*"

18 FEARLESS

The bear licketh her whelps into form, and loveth them beyond measure, and is most fierce, roaring and raging when she is robbed of them.
ARISTOTLE

Fear. It is an unsettled feeling you get in the pit of your stomach, an intense uneasiness, an acute sense of dread. Like when you turn around in a department store and your toddler has disappeared momentarily into the depths of a clothes rack.

Fear is when Josef came into the house on an October afternoon to tell me that the creek ice was "thick enough now." And I looked out the window and saw his footprints crossing the thin ice over a deep spot in the creek, the footprints filling with water and the entire area slowly sinking.

Fear is when Hans was eight and returned from the outhouse five minutes ahead of a wounded sow bear with two cubs.

And when Noah was an infant, not able to roll over yet (supposedly), and I put him on the bed "just for a second" while I went to get a diaper. And I heard the horrible sound of him hitting the wood floor after rolling off the bed from a height of three feet. He cried hard, which was good because that meant he probably was OK. His mommy was surely shaken up, though.

Or, that time I couldn't find Olivia and I knew that young man, the troubled one, was somewhere in the woods too.

Or, when Manfred slept in that remote cabin all alone and woke to the sound of a grizzly breathing on the porch. The bear crashed the door down flat to the floor, tearing it from its hinges. Then more breathing as Manfred awaited the bear's decision.

Or, when Manfred and Olivia came back from the highway and Manfred walked through the front door and told us *Hans is dead.* And then knowing, as the hours passed while they cut the car apart to get him out, that he was sitting there at the end of our driveway, so cold, so close, yet so far and so... Gone. And I could not help him, did not go to him, had no remedy for him. Nothing.

This is the quiet terror, the sudden blinding fear, that often gripped my heart in those early weeks after the crash...

I must help him.

I feel my body tense up even now as I write this nineteen months later. Mercifully, it passes quickly. But the instinct to protect, to grab my child from the teeth of danger is still so very strong. It makes me *fearless*, fully ready to face even that wounded sow bear with two cubs if doing so could rescue Hans. If it could undo the damage. If it would restore him to me.

I could kill that bear with my bare hands. I **want** to kill her.

For I am a mama bear, too. A wounded one.

19 DESIRES OF A MOTHER'S HEART

And this is the confidence that we have in him, that, if we ask any thing according to his will, he heareth us: And if we know that he hear us, whatsoever we ask, we know that we have the petitions that we desired of him. 1 John 5:14-15

Every prayer I have ever uttered for Hans, God has answered: Hans's heart is now pure, without spot, incorruptible, and overflowing with thankfulness. He is safe from evil influences. He has the mind of Christ. His knowledge is full, his humility is genuine. He worships with joy that has no limit. Love rules his every motive. He is content, has a servant's heart, follows hard after God. His faith has been perfected by sight. All the pleading petitions of a praying mother were granted the night Jesus took Hans home.

~~~

Where did Jesus go right after he laid aside the grave clothes and exited the tomb? He said he had not yet ascended to his Father. I like to think that maybe he went to see his mother.

KN

Weeping inconsolably beside a grave, can never give back love's vanished treasure. Nor can any blessing come out of such sadness. It does not make the heart any softer; it develops no feature of Christlikeness in the life. It only embitters our present joys and stunts the growth of all beautiful things. The graces of the heart are like flowers; they grow well only in the sunshine.

The joy set before us should shine upon our souls as the sun shines through clouds, glorifying them. We should cherish sacredly and tenderly, the memory of our Christian dead but should train ourselves to think of them as in the home of the blessed, with Christ, safely folded, waiting for us. Thus, the bright and blessed hopes of immortality should fill us with tranquility and healthy gladness as we move over the waves of trial.

We should remember that the blessings which have gone away are not all that God has for us. So the joys that have gone from our homes and our hearts are not the only joys; God has others in store just as rich as those we have lost, and in due time he will give us these to fill our emptied hands.

J.R. Miller (1840-1912)

20 HANS'S FAVORITE HYMN

We sang 'Come Thou Fount of Every Blessing' at Hans's memorial service. Surprisingly, I was able to sing, too, though my heart was splintering into little pieces. It was important to me that I sing that day. I wanted to do it for the Lord. I wanted to do it for Hans.

I prayed before the service that God would enable me to sing without choking up. He answered by placing several sisters in the Lord in seats close behind me. I could hear them harmonizing, and their sweet voices blessed and strengthened me. The pain was still fierce, but I actually enjoyed the singing!

Years ago, before Hans left us, our daughter sometimes played an arrangement of this hymn that I felt would be perfect for a future graduation ceremony for Hans, should he want one (he didn't). The tone of that particular arrangement was uplifting, optimistic, and hopeful. Yet, strangely, I would feel a little sad whenever she played it. At the time, I attributed those feelings to the sentimental nature of a mother's heart.

As it turned out, Hans got his graduation ceremony after all (his memorial service) when he graduated from Earth to Heaven, from temporal to eternal, from corruptible to incorruptible, when he safely arrived at his forever Home.

Come Thou Fount of Every Blessing
Robert Robinson (1758)

Come, Thou Fount of ev'ry blessing,
tune my heart to sing Thy grace;
streams of mercy, never ceasing,
call for songs of loudest praise.
Teach me some melodious sonnet,
sung by flaming tongues above;
Praise the mount—I'm fixed upon it—
mount of Thy redeeming love.

Here I raise mine Ebenezer;
hither by Thy help I've come;
and I hope, by Thy good pleasure,
safely to arrive at home.
Jesus sought me when a stranger,
wand'ring from the fold of God;
He, to rescue me from danger,
interposed His precious blood.

O to grace how great a debtor
daily I'm constrained to be!
Let Thy goodness, like a fetter,
bind my wand'ring heart to Thee:
prone to wander, Lord, I feel it,
prone to leave the God I love;
here's my heart, O take and seal it;
seal it for Thy courts above.

21 HOME

Hans spent most of his life right here at home in the house he grew up in. Of course, he went places and did things; he spent his first birthday in California while we were there visiting family. But, other than that, he never left Alaska. He never "got his own place"; never had to struggle to make ends meet, make a mortgage payment, get his heart broken, or get turned down for a job. He never "left home" until the evening he went to his Heavenly home. From his father's house to his Father's House. From home to Home.

> *In my Father's house are many mansions: if it were not so, I would have told you. I go to prepare a place for you. And if I go and prepare a place for you, I will come again, and receive you unto myself; that where I am, there ye may be also. John 14:2-3*

~~~

How divinely full of glory and pleasure shall that hour be when all the millions of mankind that have been redeemed by the blood of the Lamb of God shall meet together and stand around Him, with every tongue and every heart full of joy and praise! How astonishing will be the glory and the joy of that day when all the saints shall join together in one common song of gratitude and love, and of everlasting thankfulness to this Redeemer!

ISAAC WATTS

A continual looking forward to the eternal world is not a form of escapism or wishful thinking, but one of the things a Christian is meant to do.

C. S. LEWIS

If we believe heaven to be our country, it is better for us to transmit our wealth thither, than to retain it here, where we may lose it by a sudden removal.

JOHN CALVIN

Surely it is not wrong for us to think and talk about Heaven. I like to find out all I can about it. I expect to live there through all eternity. If I were going to dwell in any place in this country, if I were going to make it my home, I would inquire about its climate, about the neighbors—about everything... If soon you were going to emigrate, that is the way you would feel. Well, we are all going to emigrate in a very little while. We are going to spend eternity in another world. Is it not natural that we should... try to find out who is already there and what is the route to take?

D.L. MOODY

22 TIME, THE ENEMY?

Death is not my enemy, for Jesus defeated death forever when He rose from the grave on the third day. Death cannot keep me from Hans. No, death will reunite me with him.

And distance is not my real enemy, either. Hans's body, though inanimate, is here with us at home, buried in a spot of woods he cleared himself last summer, just thirty feet from where he last worked on his car the day of the crash. His spirit, though far, far away in the third heaven, is with the Lord. And the Lord is always near. Hans and I are together in Him, a *mystic sweet communion with those whose rest is won.*

No, my real enemy seems to be time. Time, like death, is irreversible. It is like dropping an egg on the floor; you cannot undrop an egg. Time is like an avalanche; you cannot shove it back up the mountain. An avalanche does not care about your problems. It buries your powerlessness without a thought.

For now, time is an inflexible law of nature. Clocks, calendars, and longing are its weapons. Time will not be hurried, cannot be undone. Time is non-negotiable, unsympathetic, no respecter of persons. It is relentless, unbending, merciless. Time is what separates me from Hans. I cannot speed it up. I cannot turn it back, cannot undo it. There is no re-wind, no reverse, no backspace, no delete. Time must be lived through. The pain must be lived with. The cavernous ache of endless Now. The finality is astonishing.

But time is also my friend. Unlike people, time can be depended on; nothing can stop it. Time passes; its steady pace is admirable. Time is temporary; it is an earth-space, creation-bound phenomenon. The eternal *now* of God's existence has been unfolded, stretched out and slowed for man's benefit, so that our little brains can endeavor to fathom it and operate within its vastness. Time is dispensed in comprehensible increments in accordance with the Lord's sovereign will, so that all may come to repentance. Time gives us a window of opportunity for meeting the Savior.

The end of time, which is when I will get to see Hans again, is a cool and shady rest, way beyond the horizon. It gathers at the terminus of a long, hard road that stretches endlessly before me.

But *when the trumpet of the Lord shall sound, and time shall be no more*, our Great God and Savior will come for me and our son will be with Him. Mr. Time loses in the end because at the close of every day I am one day closer to seeing Hans again. The day-to-day steadiness of the journey surprises me. I am making progress, though the waiting is hard, hard work.

It would be foolish and wrong to selfishly demand God bring Hans back *right now*. I was born in 1961. What if the Lord Jesus had come back in 1960? It would have shortened the wait for countless bereaved mothers, but I would never have become a mother at all. What if He had come back in 1994? Hans would not have been born yet. And what if He had come back in 1988? In 1988, I was not saved yet.

So, I must wait, but waiting does not have to mean stagnating. The Lord still has business to conduct in His universe. There are people yet to be born and souls yet to be saved. The time I have left is shorter than it feels; I must open my eyes and get busy. I need to see beyond the edges of this massive mountain called Grief and remember life is not all about me and my pain. I cannot let the mountain w of all that is still beautiful in the world. I must not sitting in ashes, forever in its shadow.

 oy, I need to stand strong under the crushing cataract relentlessly from Mount Grief's stony heart. Though it leaves me gasping for air as it pounds me with pain, it will not win, this mountain that pours torrents of sadness on me. Even as it crashes down upon my weary head, throwing me into the mire and holding me under as I miss my boy, by God's grace I will not capitulate. I will not surrender to Grief. I will stand up, defy the deluge, and breathe the fresh clean air of Truth.

And then, I will look up and see the sun that still shines on me, that has been shining all these months of sorrowing. I will look up and I will smile.

~~~

Sorrow makes deep scars; it writes its record ineffaceably on the heart which suffers. We really never get over our great griefs; we are never altogether the same after we have passed through them as we were before. Yet there is a humanizing and fertilizing influence in sorrow which has been rightly accepted and cheerfully borne. Indeed, they are poor who have never suffered, and have none of sorrow's marks upon them. The joy set before us should shine upon our grief as the sun shines through the clouds, glorifying them.

<div align="right">J.R. MILLER (1840-1912)</div>

23 PRECIOUS

I can truthfully say, with a hurting, but thankful heart, that the Lord is preserving me through this trial. I stand softened and malleable to his loving hand as He bathes my raw wounds with His love. I experience a heightened sensitivity to his presence in the depths of my pain. I believe I am growing in my faith and trust in Him. I understand and accept the truth that God purifies us through affliction. For the believer, suffering draws us closer to Him.

But what about Hans?

What I am having difficulty with is the thought that Hans did not live long enough to suffer hardship and affliction that would have provided the opportunity to become more Christ-like. Apparently, the Lord did not ordain this for Hans.

Hans did not have time to grow to ripe maturity in the Lord or to produce sacrificial fruit for Him. He did not have to suffer heartbreaking losses or work through the uncertainties of life while desperately leaning on the Lord for purifying strength. He did not experience privation or desolation, where there was no help other than what the Lord would provide in answer to prayer. He did not have time to lay up much treasure in Heaven.

Or did he?

I know full well that Hans is not missing out on anything. He is in the right place. His work is done, and he is Home. Much as we miss

him, we know he is complete, fulfilled, and satisfied and is e
life with his Savior, with his unborn siblings that went befc
and with his brothers and sisters in the Lord.

What I cannot know is what transpired in the spiritual realm during the last minutes of Hans's life here on the earth. With his injuries, I do not know if he was capable of conscious thought. But could it be that one does not have to be fully conscious to commune with the Lord?

As death overcomes the body, as temporal life slips away and the believer passes into life eternal, is the still small voice of the Lord the last and clearest thing a child of God hears on earth? Is our spiritual receptivity at its peak at this very moment? Despite the sirens, the shouting, the broken glass, the cold night air, was Hans keenly aware of his Lord's presence? Were his ears filled only with the voice of God? Did the Lord whisper to Hans, *I have a job for you, here is what it will cost you, are you willing?* If so, I would like to believe that Hans's heart whispered back, *Yes, Lord*.

I do not believe that Hans will suffer a loss of reward simply because his earthly life was short. His time here was relatively brief, but it was complete; therefore, there was no longer any reason for him to stay among us. Instead, it was ordained of God that Hans should continue his life in his Heavenly Father's presence.

Perhaps leaving his family so soon and so abruptly was part of some special assignment the Lord has for Hans. I do not think Hans would have volunteered to sign up for dying young in a car crash; few of us would. But he was the kind of guy that usually ended up doing jobs that nobody else wanted to do, simply because the thing needed doing and he was willing to do it. Maybe dying young was one of those jobs.

Sure, from our perspective, Hans's years were cut short. But eternal life with the Savior is exceedingly lavish compensation, and I am confident Hans has sufficient treasure stored up in Heaven.

I believe with all my heart that the Lord has a purpose for what happened to Hans. I do not need to know right now what it is because I will see the complete picture when I get to Glory. I would *like* to know now, but I do not *demand* to know now. I trust Almighty God was working the night of the crash and that He is working now. I trust He will reward Hans as He sees fit. Being present with the Lord is reward enough.

I cannot remember the source but, years ago, I heard the following quote on the radio, and it stuck with me. It was a program dealing with infant loss and miscarriage and it went something like this:

"The littlest [or shortest] life has fulfilled its purpose, if only to increase our longing for our heavenly home."

Hans's life has most definitely accomplished that. And I can't wait to hear the rest of his story.

*Precious in the sight of the LORD
is the death of his saints. Psalm 116:15*

24 BAUBLES AND TRINKETS

We cut our last Christmas tree with Hans in mid-December 2015. Usually, the spruces stay fresh and last well into January, sometimes sprouting new growth and even shedding pollen in the house. Manfred ordinarily cuts the tree and the children haul it home on a sled. But this year, Manfred's knee was giving him trouble, so Hans cut the tree for the first, last, and only time.

For some reason, this tree did not live very long. At first, it appeared to be a rather healthy and vigorous tree, but long before January 11, which was the day Hans drove to the highway for the last time, the tree was dropping brown needles. We took the Christmas tree down the day after the crash, on January 12, 2016—Hans's birthday, his twenty-first birthday, which he celebrated in Heaven.

Hans's Christmas tree is still out behind our house, on top of a brush pile next to the trail along the creek. His birthday presents still lay wrapped on his shelf in the boys' room. Except for the Filson shirt. We buried him in the Filson shirt. We thought, since he was turning twenty-one, we would splurge a little. On the morning of the crash, we leisurely took our time at the gun store down in Wasilla, picking out his gifts and trying to decide if we really should spend that much for a shirt. We did not know he had only hours to live or that we would see his face only one more time and just for a few minutes.

So, almost eleven months later, still unwrapped, are: an electric boot dryer, an electrical gadget that I do not even know what it is, and some other automotive thing Manfred bought for him. And a Green & Black's chocolate bar that Noah got him, which still hides in a brown paper bag waiting for someone to eat it.

Hans's Christmas presents are also on the shelf alongside his birthday gifts: a micrometer, a chainsaw tool kit you wear on your belt, a chamois car polishing sponge, all unused and all opened on Christmas morning when we had no idea he had only seventeen more days to live. However, the Glen Miller CD I gave him he enjoyed every single one of those seventeen days.

Hans does not care at all today about missing his birthday or about unopened presents. Now, eleven months later (our time), Hans is joy-struck, blown away by the magnificence of God's glory and by the wonders of His Heaven. He certainly has no need of an electric boot dryer, a micrometer, a chamois car-polishing sponge, or even chocolate.

January 3, 2016

Bells Across the Snow
Frances Ridley Havergal (1836-1879)

O Christmas, merry Christmas,
Is it really come again?
With its memories and greetings,
With its joy and with its pain!
There's a minor in the carol
And a shadow in the light,
And a spray of cypress twining
With the holly wreath tonight.
And the hush is never broken
By laughter light and low,
As we listen in the starlight
To the "bells across the snow."

O Christmas, merry Christmas,
'Tis not so very long
Since other voices blended
With the carol and the song!
If we could but hear them singing,
As they are singing now,
If we could but see the radiance
Of the crown on each dear brow,
There would be no sigh to smother,
No hidden tear to flow,
As we listen in the starlight
To the "bells across the snow."

O Christmas, merry Christmas,
This never more can be;
We cannot bring again the days
Of our unshadowed glee,
But Christmas, happy Christmas,
Sweet herald of good will,
With holy songs of glory
Brings holy gladness still.

For peace and hope may brighten,
And patient love may glow,
As we listen in the starlight
To the "bells across the snow."

25 CHRISTMAS PRAYER

At Christmastime each year, Manfred always takes our children off into the woods to find a Christmas tree while I stay back at the house and unpack the ornaments. I will arrange a few decorations, put on some Christmas music, and get the nativity set out for Josef to set up. Then, while waiting for them to return with a young spruce that is usually way too large, I will take some time to reflect over the past year and to pray for Manfred and for each of the children individually. I ponder how blessed we have been and think about what the upcoming year might hold. As the children got older, I often thought, *this may be the last Christmas we are all together. Maybe one of them will marry or get a job far away.* But each year, here we all were again. Together.

Last year's Christmas tree-cutting day, which was a few weeks before Hans left us for Heaven, as I prayed for my family, I had an awareness that the coming year might hold a special challenge for us. I felt slightly apprehensive. But, well, you know how mothers are; we always think like that. *You never know.*

So, I prayed, "Whatever it is, Lord, please be with us."

And so He has.

26 VERIFIED

*And they that know thy name will put their trust in
thee: for thou, LORD, hast not forsaken them that
seek thee. Psalm 9:10*

It is during the hard seasons of life that one finds out what kind of god one has. I want to go on record as saying that the God of the Bible, our Lord and Savior Jesus Christ, is Faithful and True and is abundantly able to give comfort and peace in the midst of anguish.

*I will not leave you comfortless:
I will come to you. John 14:18*

And, I want you to know that, despite what you think you know about Him, or what you may have been told about Him, or what they say about Him on television or social media, Jesus is God, and the Bible is God's Word to man.

And it is all True. Everything written in the Bible about God and sung about in the great hymns of the faith: His attributes. His power. His love. The promises. It is all true. Every bit of it.

*He healeth the broken in heart, and bindeth up
their wounds. Psalm 147:3*

God, Thou Art Love

If I forget,
Yet God remembers! If these hands of mine
Cease from their clinging, yet the hands divine
Hold me so firmly that I cannot fall;
And if sometimes I am too tired to call
For Him to help me, then He reads the prayer
Unspoken in my heart, and lifts my care.

I dare not fear, since certainly I know
That I am in God's keeping, shielded so
From all that else would harm, and in His power;
I tread no path in life to Him unknown;
Lift no burden, bear no pain, alone.
My soul a calm, sure hiding place has found:
The arms my life surround.

God, Thou art love! I build my faith on that.
I know Thee who has kept my path and made
Light for me in the darkness, tempering sorrow
So that it reached me like a solemn joy;
It were too strange that I should doubt Thy love.

Robert Browning

27 COURAGEOUS

Eight days before Hans died, in Sunday morning worship at church, we sang the hymn "More Love to Thee" by Elizabeth Prentiss, who lost two children and wrote this hymn while deep in her grief. It has always been a challenge for me to sing this hymn honestly and I often hesitate when beginning verse three, which in our hymnbook reads:

> *Let sorrow do its work,*
> *Send grief and pain;*
> *Sweet are Thy messengers,*
> *Sweet their refrain,*
> *When they can sing with me,*
> *More love, O Christ to Thee,*
> *More love to Thee,*
> *More love to Thee!*

Understandably, I have never sung these lines with gusto; it feels too much like lying. *Send grief and pain?!* Of course, I understand and accept the benefits to be won through trials and affliction. But to *ask* for it? I am not that brave.

I sang it anyway that last Sunday morning with my husband and all three of our sons. (Our daughter was working away from home.) I even sang verse three, but I sang it cautiously, hoping God would send no such thing.

But He did send it. He sent the sweet messengers of grief and pain, and tears, and choking sorrow. Heavy, heavy things I can accept from no other hand than that of my Father in Heaven who loves me. He has given what is best.

So, will the blessings to be gained through this present trial give me courage to ask Him to send *more* grief and *more* pain? I honestly do not think so. My entire body tenses up just thinking about it. Is anyone ever that brave?

I do not think I will have that kind of courage any time soon. Truthfully, I do not feel like being brave at all today. I confess to wanting the growth and the blessings, without the trials. If More Love means More Pain, I confess to not wanting to sign up for that right now.

Help me, Lord, to be willing to rest in whatever brings me closer to you. Help me, Lord, to be courageous.

~~~

A soldier said, "When I die do not sound taps over my grave, but reveillé, the morning call, the summons to rise."

More Love to Thee (Vs. 1,2,4)
Lyrics: Elizabeth Prentiss, (1818-1878)
Music: William Doane, (1832-1915)

More love to Thee, O Christ,
More love to Thee!
Hear Thou the prayer I make
On bended knee;
This is my earnest plea:
More love, O Christ, to Thee,
More love to Thee,
More love to Thee!

Once earthly joy I craved,
Sought peace and rest;
Now Thee alone I seek,
Give what is best;
This all my prayer shall be:
More love, O Christ, to Thee,
More love to Thee,
More love to Thee!

Then shall my latest breath
Whisper Thy praise;
This be the parting cry
My heart shall raise;
This still its prayer shall be:
More love, O Christ, to Thee,
More love to Thee,
More love to Thee!

28 THOUGHTS ON PSALM 84

PSALM 84
To the chief Musician upon Gittith,
A Psalm for the sons of Korah.

1 How amiable are thy tabernacles,
O LORD of hosts!

Hans was happy at home. He loved this place, our little log tabernacle in the woods, the land, the creek, the surrounding fields and forests. And though he and Manfred attended other churches when they were working out of town, the Bible Church in Nenana was the only church home Hans ever knew.

But, lovely as our home is here on the earth, and precious as the fellowship is which we enjoy with the saints in that little church, these are but a taste, a shadow of what we will experience when we get to God's Heaven. They cannot compare with what Hans is experiencing right now. *He is with Almighty God!* The Lord of all the universe and beyond. The Maker of Heaven and Earth.

2 My soul longeth, yea, even fainteth for the courts
of the LORD: my heart and my flesh crieth out for
the living God.

Since Hans went to be with the Lord Jesus, I confess I have been longing for Hans more than for the living God. My heart and my flesh have been crying out for Hans; to see him, to hear him, to grab hold of him. My eagerness to enter the courts of the Lord has been so I could be with Hans again.

I guess for a mother this is understandable, and I have not beaten myself up too much about it. But the time has come for me to move beyond it. I am not asking the Lord to remove my longing for Hans, but that this longing for our son would not eclipse the longing for my Savior. I ask that He increase my longing for the living God, the God of the living, Hans's God, my God. The God in whose presence Hans now lives.

> *3 Yea, the sparrow hath found an house, and the swallow a nest for herself, where she may lay her young, even thine altars, O LORD of hosts, my King, and my God.*

For the last ten years of his life, Hans slept on the top bunk of a triple bunk bed he shared with his two brothers. From this lofty perch, with its commanding view of the entire house (it's a small house), Hans presided over many shenanigans. On the exterior side of the log wall, behind the head-end of Hans's third-tier bed, attached to the outside of the house, just a few feet from where Hans rested his head at night, is a birdhouse. It is a house made specifically for the swallows that return here each year in the spring. Hans grew up listening to the swallows build their nests and raise their young every year. The peeping sometimes kept him awake.

On the night Hans died, before we knew anything for certain, and as my uneasiness grew, I began preparing to go to the hospital. All we knew was that Hans was overdue, and there was a wreck on the highway at the end of our road. Was he hurt, or was he on the scene responding as a medic?

There I sat alone, waiting for someone to walk back from the highway and tell me what was going on. And then my eye fell on the December newsletter from Slavic Gospel Association, lying on the end table. The cover article headline read:

> *"Lord, if you want me to lay my son on the altar, I will."*

I rose and went to our bedroom, slowly closing the door behind me. By the bedside, I prayed and calmly laid our son on the altar.

I did not like doing it. I cannot say my heart was in it. But I did it. I was not a cheerful giver, but neither did I give him up grudgingly. I felt a sense of foreboding, but there was no struggle. I believed it was what I needed to do. Because that was the only thing *to* do. The altar was the safest place for Hans to be.

Even as I gave him up, I did not really believe God would take Hans from us. Our house, with its swallow nest and the bier upon which Hans slept, had become an altar, had always been an altar. I just never knew it before.

> *4 Blessed are they that dwell in thy house: they will be still praising thee. Selah.*

This is what Hans is doing *right now*. He is praising God. If I want to be near Hans, this is the best way I can think of—*praise God*. *Selah*, pause and meditate on dwelling with God and praising Him for all eternity.

> *5 Blessed is the man whose strength is in thee; in whose heart are the ways of them.*

This is what you must understand who say to me: "You are so strong; God knows who to give his troubles to; I couldn't do it; Your religion will help you get through this; God never gives us more than we can handle." *This is very important for you to get*: I am not strong; God has no troubles; you could do it if you had to; "religion" has nothing to do with it; and I most definitely have been given more than I can handle. Any strength you think you see in me is the LORD. And if I do not follow Him, especially during this sorrowful time, I will sink into a heap of despair and pain from which it would be very difficult to recover.

> *6 Who passing through the valley of Baca make it a well; the rain also filleth the pools.*

The valley of Baca—the valley of Weeping—this is where I am. A dry place one must pass through on the way to the Lord's house. But the verse says *passing through*. If I look for them through my tears, showers of blessing will fill the pools, diluting my sorrow and watering my spirit, so that fruit may increase and ripen.

> *7 They go from strength to strength, every one of them in Zion appeareth before God.*

Every wave of sorrow given over to Him with rejoicing, strengthens me and enables me to move forward until at last I will appear before God.

> *8 O LORD God of hosts, hear my prayer: give ear, O God of Jacob. Selah.*

He has heard; He hears now; He will hear always.

> *9 Behold, O God our shield, and look upon the face of thine anointed.*

When I am weak with longing and sorrow, my God shields me from the enemy, from Satan, who would love to see me doubt God's goodness and promises. By God's grace, this I will not do.

> *10 For a day in thy courts is better than a thousand. I had rather be a doorkeeper in the house of my God, than to dwell in the tents of wickedness.*

Just one day with God in glory is better than a thousand blessed days down here on the earth. A day with Him in Heaven is jam-packed with unimaginable blessing. The beauty of *here* is just a shadow, is embryonic. The wonders of *there* are beyond our perception. There can be no comparison—our understanding is far too limited.

For about a year and a half, Hans led the singing on Sunday mornings at our church, "just a number caller-outer" as he put it. This placed him well outside his comfort zone, as he strongly preferred a background roll. He did not enjoy public speaking and possessed no musical inclinations. He was a hard worker and gave of his time in helping with repairing, renovating, and maintaining the church building—a doorkeeper, if you will. I fully expect to see Hans at the gate of Heaven when I arrive, eager to share what he has been up to, to show me how much better God's plan was in keeping him far from the tents of wickedness.

> *11 For the LORD God is a sun and shield: the LORD will give grace and glory: no good thing will he withhold from them that walk uprightly.*

Hans was far from perfect, but he was a young man who walked uprightly, by God's grace. In cutting his earthly life short, God has withheld no good thing from our Hans. For the Christian, to die is gain, and Hans has surely gotten the better end of the deal. He is basking in the light of God's presence, utterly shielded from all evil, rich with the benefits and blessings of God's grace. Engulfed in His glory.

> *12 O LORD of hosts, blessed is the man that trusteth in thee.*

In fierce storms, said an old seaman, we must do one thing; there is only one way: we must put the ship in a certain position and keep her there. This, Christian, is what you must do. Sometimes, like Paul, you can see neither sun nor stars, and no small tempest lies on you; and then you can do but one thing; there is only one way. Reason cannot help you; past experiences give you no light. Even prayer fetches no consolation. Only a single course is left—you must put your soul in one position and keep it there. You must stay upon the Lord; and come what may—winds, waves, cross-seas, thunder, lightning, frowning rocks, roaring breakers—no matter what, you must lash yourself to the helm, and hold fast your confidence in God's faithfulness, His covenant engagement, His everlasting love in Christ Jesus.

RICHARD FULLER (1804-1876)

29 CLEANING HOUSE

I wrote this chapter on a rather tough day. I needed to get it onto paper and out of my heart. I was not going to publish it, but maybe it will help someone.

Why I Do Not Want to Move On.
Why I Do Not Want to Let Him Go...

Letting go and moving on is not something I want to do. I just can't. Pain is something I have always avoided, and most normal people will do almost anything to keep from experiencing pain. But *this* pain I do not seek to get away from. Grief does not follow the rules of logic.

Why do I hold so tightly to it? Why do I continually live in the past and replay old memories? Why do I seek to stay in a place of pain? Why do I feel as though existing in a state of emotional anguish keeps me closer to him? Why do I keep his things around and pretend he is still here or that he might be home soon?

I just do. That's how it is. It has been ten months? Ten months means nothing. For me it is still January 11, 2016, 6:05 p.m.

Why do I stay sad? Somebody has to. He was not a lost set of keys, or a barn that burned down. He was our son, our first son. With him went a daughter-in-law that never was, and I have been praying all these years for a young lady that never even existed. Gone are maybe half a dozen grandchildren we will never hold. He was a guardian for his disabled brother, a friend and protector for his sister, a companion and comrade to his brothers, a provider for when we are old. We have lost so very much more than one person. We were so proud of him for all he was and all we hoped he would be. He made us laugh. And he is gone. It is all gone.

I do not want to smile. I do not want to talk. I do not want to be happy. I want my son. I do not want to get over it, move on, let him go, or feel better. This is not logical. I want the pain to be gone, but I do not want to let go of the pain. I do not want to let go of my son. Letting him go feels like leaving him on a doorstep or putting him in a basket and floating him down the Nile. I do not want to say goodbye. I wish I could have said goodbye. I want him back. I want him to be happy. He *is* happy. I am unhappy that he is gone, but being gone has made him happy. Am I really this selfish? What kind of mother am I?

Oh, troubled heart, be still and learn that no selfishness can be in love; that he who loves his Master withholds nothing when He has need of it; and he who loves his child will sink all sense of loss in the everlasting gain of lying safe upon the bosom of the Shepherd.

BENJAMIN PALMER

To be happy seems to be the same as saying that I have nothing to be sad about. Happiness seems to diminish our son's value. People who have not expressed sorrow at our loss seem to convey that we did not lose much. I know they do not really think this, but that is how it feels. I know they are afraid of upsetting me, but it is unlikely that I could be more upset than I am already. Acting as if Hans never existed does not help me. It is an outrage, and there is no more effective way to wound me further. He not only existed, but he exists even now with the Lord. I need to be reminded of this even though I know it is true and I am hanging on to this truth with everything I've got.

So what if I cry? Cry with me. There are some that have not shed one tear in my presence, have not shared one memory of our son, have not spoken his name—not once. Our eye doctor cried, our customers cried, our mechanic's wife cried. But others, who I thought would understand or at least attempt to try, gave me canned, platitudinous, generic comfortisms. I could have just bought myself a Hallmark™ card.

I do not want to talk about me and How I Am Doing. I want to hear you talk about Hans, and I want you to talk about him because you miss him, too—not because you know it is what I want and need to hear.

And you there, the ones who should have thought before speaking, in answer to your incredible questions: *Yes, forever.* And *Yeah, somebody died.*

I am not angry with God. Not even one little bit. I am angry with death and with time and with thoughtless people; people who say nothing, who will not weep with those who weep. I understand your discomfort, but your heartfelt tears would mean so much to me. If you want to do something for me, remember our son. And then tell me about it. It just might help.

POSTSCRIPT: So, there was some bitterness here. I have confessed and forsaken it. The anger is gone. I have asked the Lord to help me be merciful and gentle with people. I have forgiven offenses, real and imagined. Most of us have so little experience with comforting the grieving. I used to be one of those who did not know what to do with a person like me. Because there really is nothing you *can* do. No one can fix this.

I have asked my Father in Heaven to not let me become damaged, joyless, useless. The pain leaves one so vulnerable. So tired.

But God is good, and I trust Him. I trust Him fully and more completely than ever. The absolute sure hope of Heaven has never been more real to me.

I can rejoice in that. Thank God.

~~~

Grief is suspicious of gladness and is slow to be persuaded that he who comes to the house of mourning from the dwelling of cheerfulness can bring with him a just appreciation of the calamity which he seeks to soothe. To be able to weep with those who weep, is a necessary prerequisite in one who would be, in the divine sense, a son of consolation.
Charles J. Vaughan (1816-1897)

While grief is fresh, every attempt to divert only irritates. You must wait till it be digested, and then amusement will dissipate the remains of it.
Samuel Johnson

His son will soon have been dead a week, and he has not really talked to anybody yet. He wants to talk of it properly, with deliberation. He wants to tell how his son was taken ill, how he suffered, what he said before he died, how he died. He wants to describe the funeral, and how he went to the hospital to get his son's clothes... Yes, he has plenty to talk about now. His listener ought to sigh and exclaim and lament. It would be even better to talk to women. Though they are silly creatures, they blubber at the first word.
-From 'Misery', Anton Pavlovich Chekhov (1860-1904)

30 ACCIDENT OR APPOINTMENT?

... this thing is from me. 1 Kings 12:24

Did God take our son, or was it an accident? It depends on what you mean by "accident." Was the crash unexpected, unintentional, unplanned? Yes, from our earthbound perspective, but not to God. The Lord was not caught off guard or taken by surprise on the night of the crash. Was the crash without divine cause or influence? Was it preventable, random, avoidable, mere chance, coincidence, bad luck, just one of those things? No, it was not.

We use this word "accident" all the time and the inevitable should-haves and if-onlys follow close behind:

A young man is killed in a car crash, an MVA, a Motor Vehicle Accident. If only he had stayed home that night.

The girl breaks her leg in three places while skiing; what a terrible accident. She should have stayed on the beginner hill like I told her.

I drop a pie on the floor; what a clumsy accident. If only you had not bumped into me. Oops.

A man of God is arrested, is shipwrecked with a bunch of convicts and then gets bit by a snake. Apparently, this man has experienced a series of unfortunate accidents. Perhaps he should have been more careful?

Here is one of those eighth-grade math word problems for you: A young man driving a car is proceeding along a dirt road toward a rural two-lane highway. His speed is between five and ten miles per hour. At the same time, a pickup truck is traveling this same rural highway toward the very spot where the young man is about to emerge from the dirt driveway. The pickup is going between fifty-five and sixty-five miles per hour. It is dark, and the roads are frosty. They are on a collision course, but before the pickup can plow into the driver's door of the young man's car, there are many things that must happen first. If anything should delay or speed up any of those things, the two vehicles will not meet.

This would include things like: If either driver accelerates, even minutely, or eases his foot off the gas slightly while reaching for the radio; or sneezes; or puts fuel in the tank before leaving town, enters the wrong PIN at the pump and must re-enter it; or stops by the side of the road to use the facilities, etc. If any task or communication takes slightly more or less time at any moment of that entire day, the vehicles will not meet at the end of the driveway. What is the probability that the two vehicles will collide?

I think it is safe to say the number of factors that need to be lined up in perfect order for these two vehicles to meet is incalculable, maybe infinite. I wish some mathematician would figure out the "chances" of something like this happening.

Consider this: according to Henry Morris (The Henry Morris Study Bible, New Leaf Publishers ©1995 used with permission)

> "The probability that eleven men [Joseph's brothers in Genesis Chapter 43] could be 'accidentally' arranged in order of age is only one chance out of 39,917,000... there are almost forty million ways in which eleven men could be seated."

I am positive there are far more than eleven variables that come into play when trying to figure out the chances of that exact pickup hitting Hans's car on that particular night and hitting it precisely where it would do the most damage.

But, since the Biblical Joseph knew the ages of his brothers, seating them according to their ages was not a problem for him. The brothers, not having complete knowledge of the situation (they did not yet recognize Joseph), *marveled. What an incredible coincidence to be seated that way "by accident."*

Incredible? Yes. Accident? Coincidence? No. Joseph possessed knowledge his brothers were not privy to yet. He arranged their seating for his own purposes, just as God allowed the brothers to fake Joseph's death and sell him to a passing caravan whose travel schedule God had pre-arranged. They thought to do evil, but God meant it for good.

It is not that they did evil, and then God figured out a way to make their evil actions work out later for good. God was directing events, but the brothers are still responsible for choosing to do evil. God allowed them to choose to do what they wanted to do. They did evil and God allowed them to do it because their actions put Joseph where God wanted him to be. I do not have perfect knowledge of all of life's contingencies. But God does, and He allows or arranges all that happens for His good purposes.

To me, the best use of this word *accident* is to make sure people know I did not do something on purpose: *Sorry about your toe, I stepped on it by accident.* Accidents are usually someone's fault. They are unintended events due to carelessness, poor judgement, defective equipment, etc. So, in that sense, the crash that ended Han's earthly life was an accident, something unplanned and unforeseen. Hans's big snow boot got wedged behind the brake pedal, making it impossible for him to stop the car sufficiently when he reached the highway, and this resulted in an accident.

But leaving God out of it and classifying it exclusively as a chance event, a coincidence, a natural outcome of the laws of physics, bad luck, an unfortunate choice, pilot error or just a bad break makes me uncomfortable. It trivializes the whole horrible thing and seems to imply that God was not paying attention or that life is a throw of the dice, or that we are at the mercy of our own fallibility and the universe's rigid natural laws over which God has no control, that there is no purpose for what happened. *Stuff happens—It was just an accident.*

Perhaps it happened by chance or natural laws, and then God used it for His purposes after the fact? It seems to me that, while it is true God can use any "random" event for His glory and our good, this way of thinking is akin to the idea that God created the universe but then things went terribly wrong, and He has been wringing His hands trying to get something good to come out of it ever since.

The fact is that God could easily have kept Hans from driving to the highway. God could have kept Hans from dying. But He did not. I am one of those folks that believes God either causes or allows everything that comes to pass. The sparrow that falls to the ground, the wipe-out on the ski hill, the shipwreck, the snake, the pie, the crash—everything. *God has His universe under control.* God does not do evil. God is good. But He allows sinful man a lot of freedom to prove his utter hopelessness apart from his Creator and Sustainer—and sometimes that gets ugly.

Some say God never violates our free will. I thank God that He can and will overrule our choices if it suits His purposes. I rejoice He freed my self-loving will when He saved me from bondage to sin. Choices have consequences, but the Lord can influence our choices. He allows or enables us to choose or not to choose. He is in charge, not us. He has ordained that sorrow and evil are permitted for a season. This does nothing to taint His character. He is not obligated to explain Himself to us.

God is good and does good. He is merciful and in control of His universe. Trusting Him is the only way I can manage this pain. I think the difficulty for some comes when the loss occurs through events such as long-term illness, murder, or suicide rather than by an "accident." Understandably, it is much harder to see any "good" *at all* connected with such things. Death is ugly. The horror and evil that is instrumental in the death of some of our loved ones is part of the groaning fallenness of our world. These things are not good. It is GOD that is good, and He will redeem and restore *all* things. He will make it right. His children have nothing to fear.

I am moved by the heartbreaking anguish of parents who question: *Why did this happen? Was it 'just an accident'? If I had been more careful, might this accident not have happened? What could have been done to produce a different outcome?*

Grieving, suffering mother, you could spend a lifetime replaying all the possibilities and get nowhere. Thrashing about in the tar pit of *What if?* is a futility that will eventually swallow you up.

But here is the good news: God has all those what-ifs, I-should-haves, why-didn't-yous covered. And He can override our mistakes, our stupidities, and yes, even our diligent care to bring about the purposes He has ordained. God was in complete control the day your child died.

Many bereaved parents cannot believe this. They can see no acceptable reason for God to allow such heartbreak and therefore believe there must be no value or purpose in it. Second causes are elevated above the Sovereign Lord, who alone has the final say over all that will or will not take place.

It is easy to regard the pain of child loss as the center of our universe, a fallen universe swirling in chaos around our broken heart. While this is a perfectly normal way to feel, if fed and perpetuated, it can lead to wrong thinking, and wrong thinking compounds our pain. For example:

God did not take my child. Satan took my child and God did not or could not stop it. The way I see it, if God did not take Hans, then Satan won on January 11, 2016—he successfully took out a young man with great potential for service to the Lord. However, Hans belongs to Jesus and Satan can do nothing God does not allow. God is the ultimate authority.

> How frequently God's saints see only Satan as the cause of their troubles. They regard the great enemy as responsible for much of their sufferings. But there is no comfort for the heart in this. We do not deny that the Devil does bring about much that harasses us. But above Satan is the Lord Almighty! The Devil cannot touch a hair of our heads without God's permission, and when he is allowed to disturb and distract us, even then it is only God using him to try us. Let us learn then, to look beyond all secondary causes and instruments to that One who worketh all things after the counsel of His own will (Eph. 1:11)
>
> A.W. Pink
> *Comfort for Christians*

On the night of Hans's crash, God had the final say, not Satan. And not only will our Father redeem this loss for our good and His glory, but from it He can and will deliver a perfect and total victory in ways that we cannot imagine—ways that were ordained before the foundation of the world. I could not accept such a devastating loss from any other hand than that of my Savior who loves me.

God doesn't kill people. Certainly not 'good' people. It was just an accident. The fact is, God brought about the death of His very own son—*for you.*

> *Yet it pleased the LORD to bruise him; he hath put him to grief: Isaiah 53:10*

If God is good, He would not have allowed my child to die. Or, in other words, God is only good if He gives me what I want or exempts me from heartache. This is a very self-centered way of viewing God. People die every day. There is sin and suffering all over the world; why should God exempt *me*? Did He ever promise to spare his children from pain? Do I deserve a better deal than countless hurting people throughout the ages?

There is a bigger picture to consider that goes beyond my own personal pain. Just because death brings sadness does not mean God is not good. Would God be good if everyone lived forever, if all tears were wiped away, if everything wrong was made right? Would that meet your expectations? Well, here is good news: God has made provision for all of that in His Son, Jesus Christ:

> *Jesus said unto her, I am the resurrection, and the life: he that believeth in me, though he were dead, yet shall he live: And whosoever liveth and believeth in me shall never die. Believest thou this? John 11:25,26*

> *And God shall wipe away all tears from their eyes; and there shall be no more death, neither sorrow, nor crying, neither shall there be any more pain: for the former things are passed away. Revelation 21:4*

This world is not all there is. There is a wonderful plan unfolding before our eyes and only God knows all the details. But there is also a lot of stuff going on down here that is beyond horrendous. Thank God this is not all there is. How could we bear it? Why would we?

So where is God? Why doesn't He stop the suffering? What kind of God lets a baby die? Or maybe He is not powerful enough to keep evil in check. Maybe He does not care about me. *Where was Jesus when my child died?*

Dear suffering one, He was and is on His throne. He sees it all. No one gets away with anything. No matter how dreadful the circumstances regarding the death of your child, He will someday make all things right and beautiful when He returns. For those who belong to Him, when we see Him face to face, we will be completely satisfied and convinced of the rightness of His plan. There will be justice. There will be restoration. There will be healing. But in His time.

I know. You want it now. Me, too. But this is where trust comes in. God sees the complete picture, and He knows everything about everything and everyone. He knows what is best in all circumstances. He knows what He is doing. He is God.

So, did God take Hans? Was it an accident or was it an Appointment? Many people think it was an accident, a tragedy, something that should not have happened. Honestly, I wish it had not. But it all depends on your perspective. If this life is all there is, then it was a tragedy, an irredeemable loss. A terrible accident.

But if this life is just a vapor (and it is); and if there is an all-powerful, all-knowing God of love who is preparing an eternal home for me (and there is); if, in His wisdom, He causes or allows painful things to happen in order to accomplish His wider purpose, (it really isn't all about me, after all), then I can count everything that happens to me a victory. In Him, I am free from the torment of what-ifs and I can view Hans's home-going as an Appointment with Almighty God, an event of great significance in God's plan. But to realize this, I must do one thing: I must believe Him.

~~~

Blessed is that man who is done with chance, who never speaks of luck—but believes that from the least, even to the greatest, all things are ordained by the Lord. We dare not leave out the least event! The creeping of an aphid upon a rosebud is as surely arranged by the decree of Providence as the march of a pestilence through a nation! Believe this, for if the least thing is omitted from the supreme government, so may the next be, and the next – until nothing is left in the divine hands. There is no place for chance, since God fills all things.

CHARLES SPURGEON

We talk of God's providence when we have hairbreadth escapes. But are they not quite as much divine providences, when we are [or are not] preserved from danger?

CHARLES SPURGEON

There is no such thing as chance, luck or accident in the Christian journey through this world. All is arranged and appointed by God. And all things are working together for the believer's good!

J. C. RYLE

31 MAMA

In the 1948 movie, *I Remember Mama*, there is a sequence where the youngest child needs an operation. The mother promises the child to be there at the hospital when the little girl wakes up. Later, after the successful operation is concluded, the mother discovers there is a rule that forbids visitors in the first twenty-four hours after surgery. But Mother has promised to come; the child is calling for her in the night, *Mama. Mama.*

It is heartrending to watch this mother as she tries to get to her child without being caught by the nurses. Finally, she poses as a cleaning woman and, on her knees, scrubs her way to the ward where she finds her child calling for her. She comforts the child and slips away, promise kept.

If you have ever been separated from your child when she needed you; if you have ever heard him cry out in pain and you were powerless to relieve it. If you have ever gazed upon your child's lifeless body and tried to will it back to life with the force of your love, then you know what it is to have your heart pierced. No, not pierced... *Demolished.*

A mother's compulsion to protect her child from danger is intense. We do not lose this instinct when the child grows up, or moves away, or dies. It is an agony when our help becomes an impossibility.

When your child is abruptly torn from you, the sense of powerlessness, the utter inability to affect a rescue, is an ocean falling on top of you. It is an Engulfment, and nothing less than holding that child and making it all better will assuage it.

I count it an honor and a great blessing to be a Mommy, though Death of a Child is one part of motherhood I never thought I would experience, would rather not experience.

But I would do it all again in a heartbeat.

~~~

Few bereavements cause more sorrow and disappointment, than when little children die. But even in these, there are consolations. That the baby came at all, was a blessing. Life was never the same in the home after that, never could be the same; it had in it a new element of blessing. Then its stay, whether it was for one day, one month, or a year, was like the tarrying of a heavenly messenger. Nothing can ever rob the home of the blessings it left there in its brief stay.

J. R. Miller 1896

32 "I'LL BE RIGHT BACK."

The other night in prayer meeting, we were taking turns reading scripture. We went around the group and when my turn came, I was asked to read from the Gospel of John, chapter eleven, verses twenty-five and twenty-six:

> *Jesus said unto her, I am the resurrection, and the life: he that believeth in me, though he were dead, yet shall he live: And whosoever liveth and believeth in me shall never die. Believest thou this?*

With some advanced warning, I probably would have been fine but, being caught unprepared, I could barely get through the whole verse without choking up. How could I not weep reading Jesus' words to Martha? For these are the very words inscribed on the back of Hans's gravestone. Below this verse are his last words to us,

"I'll be right back."

John 11:25-26 is the focal point of my faith right now. It is the promise I grab hold of every time missing Hans becomes unbearable. *Without this promise, I would never see our son again.* Christ's resurrection is a promise of victory over death and the grave for all who know Jesus as Lord and Savior.

Hans's physical body is here with us. I can look out my window and see where it is buried. From that very spot, Hans will come up out of the ground clothed with a new, indestructible body. We will join the Lord in the air and be together forever—*Jesus said so.* Let us look at this word *resurrection.*

> Resurrection: (Webster's Revised Unabridged Dictionary) 1. (n.) A rising again; a return from death to life; as the resurrection of Christ. 2. (n.) Especially, the rising again from the dead; the resumption of life by the dead; as, the resurrection of Jesus Christ; the general resurrection of all the dead at the Day of Judgment.

Jesus Christ's literal, actual, physical, bodily resurrection is the very foundation of Christianity. Because Jesus rose from the dead, we have a guarantee of the future resurrection of all believers. That includes Hans. Wishful thinking is not enough. If Christ did not come out of that tomb alive, if the resurrection is not an historical fact, we have nothing, and our faith is a cruel delusion.

> *And if Christ be not raised, your faith is vain; ye are yet in your sins. Then they also which are fallen asleep in Christ are perished. If in this life only we have hope in Christ, we are of all men most miserable. 1 Corinthians 15:17-19*

If Jesus rose from the dead, then everything he said is true; and if he did not rise from the dead, it is false. In addition, the resurrection of the dead will be for both the just and the unjust (Dan. 12:2; John 5:28,29; Romans 2:6-16; 2 Thessalonians 1:6-10). Furthermore, our resurrection body will differ from the body which was laid to rest in the grave. (1 Corinthians 15:53,54; Philippians 3:21). Its identity, however, will be maintained—we will know each other. It will still be the same body (1 Corinthians 15:42-44); but transformed into a new and perfected body—whole, healthy, powerful, beautiful.

I not only believe this. I *know* it is true.

33 BLIND-SIDED AT SEARS

Walking through the Sears department store one afternoon, as I passed through the boys' and then the men's department, I calmly experienced all the expected memories: the packages of socks, the work pants, the plaid shirts, the dress shirts, the glass elevator our boys liked to use as an observation tower while I shopped for their Christmas presents.

Continuing on through the tool department, where we bought so many gifts for the men in our family—the flashlights, the socket wrench sets, the tool bags, I was feeling rather victorious, thinking I had handled all that pretty well. Feeling safe, I headed for housewares to look at sheets but then found myself in the little girls' department, which comes just before housewares. For some reason, I suddenly felt uneasy. But what on earth could be safer than the little girls' department?

I ignored the silent warning, which told me to just look straight ahead and press on to housewares. Instead, I let my eyes swing to the left to look at the little girls' dresses, all pink and frilly and loaded with ribbons. So girly. No little boy memories here.

So why the tears out of nowhere, in the very center of Sears department store, far from the exit or even a bathroom where I might hide and compose myself? Why this sudden clutching heaviness in my heart for no apparent reason? Because there is a reason. Hans will never have a little girl. Never.

And he would have been such a great Daddy.

Manfred holding Hans, one day old

34 THOUGHTS ON PSALM 55

> *My heart is sore pained within me: and the terrors of death are fallen upon me. Fearfulness and trembling are come upon me, and horror hath overwhelmed me. Psalm 55:4,5*

This is not happening…

The men from our church placed two stout spruce poles across the open grave, the silent hole in the frozen ground where they intended to put our son. They slid the casket onto the poles and retreated, leaving it there, exposed and vulnerable, suspended over the chasm in the cold January sunlight. In silence it waited, alone, for when the men would pull the poles and lower our boy into the earth.

I looked at the dirt pile opposite me. Near it was a charred chunk of wood from the three-day fire we built to thaw the winter earth. Next to the dirt pile, in the trampled snow, was a crumpled blue tarp. *What was that doing there?* Its ordinariness was out of place; Hans might have thrown it over his tools yesterday to keep the snow off.

I glanced at our two younger sons and then at my husband as he tried to think what to do next. *How do you bury your son and your father* on the same day?* I stood beside the hole, quietly clutching the folded up American flag presented to me at the memorial service. So composed.

But inside I was screaming. *"No! Wait! What are you doing? Let's talk this over. There must be another way. You cannot put my son in there!"* It was like waiting for the trapdoor to spring at a hanging. As if the casket was putting out to sea, or launching into space, never to be seen again. As if they were getting ready to throw my little boy off a cliff. That is how it feels to bury a child.

~~~

The writings of other parents who have buried children have been of tremendous comfort to me. It is a rescue at sea to read your own heartache in the words of another; to wail through sloppy tears,

Yes, that's just how it is!

Likewise, I often find my emotions voiced perfectly in the pages of Scripture. Since Hans left us for Heaven, I have spent some time each day reading in the Psalms. Circled in my Bible are many verses that have spoken to my heart as only God's Word can. Here are a few from Psalm fifty-five:

> *Oh that I had wings like a dove!*
> *for then would I fly away, and be at rest. v. 6*

The first three nights after the crash, I did not sleep more than a few hours total. I was in complete fight-or-flight mode, adrenaline urging me to flee, to fly, to run to where Hans is. *To find him.*

I knew he was Home with the Lord and that he was safe and happy. But his body, the strong, beautiful body that used to be my little boy, was with the medical examiner in Anchorage. Then he was on a plane again, *as cargo*, back to Fairbanks. Then he was at the funeral home. *The funeral home!* These are not places you want your child to be.

One of my children is not in their bed. Why does he not come home? He always calls. Why doesn't he call? Were those his headlights shining through the window just now? **How, how, how can this be?!**

On and on through the night my heart bled, making sleep impossible. Making normal breathing impossible. *The terrors of death are fallen upon me.* The horror was overwhelming.

But I would like you to know that when we become overwhelmed with pain and grief, God can bring rest. Listen, when you read or hear about someone crying out to God in anguish (I mean literally crying out) and they say that, while praying from the depths of their despair, God gave them an immediate and profound peace—believe them. For the Lord astonished me this very way when I thought I just might really lose it—I was truly coming apart, being torn apart, with grief and longing. The pain was ferocious, eviscerating, terrifying, suffocating, and out from under it, I could whisper only two words:

Help me.

And then I felt it come. From the top of my head, the warmth poured down over me and shut my silently screaming mouth—so abruptly that I actually laughed. What had fallen upon me, displacing the terror as it enfolded me from head to foot like a soft blanket? *Peace.* The Lord was pouring peace on me. It was nearly tangible.

It was not the everything-is-fine-and-my-problems-are-all-gone kind of "peace." It was something I have never felt before. The plug had been pulled. And as the pain drained out the bottom of my soul, a holy hush took its place, filling me from the top and then running over, quenching my hot tears in an instant. It was a peace that was clearer than contentment and softer than happiness. The storm had calmed. I was in the arms of my Father.

This wonderful calm did not last as long as I would have liked. It was a kind of temporary cease-fire which allowed the women and children to exit the field of battle. But I was still. I did not return to my wailing. I was instantly "OK"—functional, composed (for real), and able to return to whatever I needed to do.

So what happened here? Just this: I had received comfort from the God of all comfort. When I most desperately needed Him, He was there, as He always is.

> *As for me, I will call upon God; and the LORD shall save me. Evening, and morning, and at noon, will I pray, and cry aloud: and he shall hear my voice.*

> *He hath delivered my soul in peace from the battle
> that was against me: v. 16-18*

If I step out my front door, walk around to the back of the house, then down the outhouse trail, over the little bridge that crosses the creek, and keep walking, I will eventually come to Siberia. Of course, I would never make it, but you get the idea. There is a wilderness out there and it will kill you if you are not careful.

> *Lo, then would I wander far off, and remain in the
> wilderness. Selah. I would hasten my escape from
> the windy storm and tempest. v. 7-8*

I thought about that—not that I wanted to die in the wilderness—but I thought, If I start walking and keep going until I am too tired to walk back, I will freeze to death. It is well below zero degrees today—I could be with Hans in less than an hour.

I in no way wanted to die—I have a wonderful family that I love. Plus, I hate to be cold (living in Alaska?!). But these are the kinds of things you think of when you are in a tempest of grief, a wild, shrieking storm of sorrow.

Friend, from the midst of your storm, call upon your Father God. He is there and ready to comfort you—just as He promised.

> *Cast thy burden upon the LORD, and he shall
> sustain thee: he shall never suffer the righteous
> to be moved. v.22*

---

*Ernst August Eduard Nolywaika 1/12/27—12/6/13. Hans and his grandfather shared a birthday but never met. I was pregnant with Hans during Ernst's final visit from Germany. The summer before the crash, Hans cleared the place on our property where we planned on burying Opa Ernst's ashes. He could not have imagined it would soon be his own resting place as well.

35 DETESTABLE TO THE LORD

I know. It hurts.

You miss him. You miss your child so terribly much. And the pain. The pain seems more than you can bear another minute. You want to see him, to hear his voice, to know where he is and if he is well and happy. But you cannot. Then someone whispers, *Yes, you can.*

Mediums, spiritualists, psychics, necromancers, diviners; readers of cards, tea leaves, and stars—who are these people and what do they offer the grieving? Unfortunately, there are many among the bereaved who seek to contact the departed by engaging the services of these occult practitioners. But I will not. Here is why:

1. God forbids it.
2. I refuse to be exploited by someone who is a fake at best and a channel for demonic entities at worst.
3. Nor will I allow someone who engages in this type of wickedness to become part of something as personal and intimate as the loss of our son. I will not have Hans's name bandied about in this manner. His memory will not be mocked in the spirit world or traded as a commodity for evil in the physical one.

4. It would be beyond horrifying to hear a demon counterfeiting the voice of our Hans.
5. I will not expose myself to or subject my family to the influence of unclean spirits.
6. "Feeling better" after being exploited like this would not help me. Allowing myself to be deceived to obtain false "comfort" is destructive, not healing.
7. I should focus on communing with my Father God, the True Comforter, not on trying to get Hans back. Why would I ask a demon for questionable information about Hans when I can have the Truth from Jesus, my Savior, the One Whom Hans is actually with?
8. Hans would not want me to.

The argument in favor of engaging the services of a medium usually goes something like this: I felt so much better afterwards. I know I talked to my deceased loved one. The psychic had very accurate information. She knew things no one else could know.

Of course she did. That is the point. This is actually worse than being duped by a skillful confidence predator. I would rather be tricked by a sneaky swindler than be in actual contact with a lying demon. You must ask: Where did this inside information come from? Since God forbids this sort of thing, He is not about to give special, private information to people who are profiting by disregarding His Word. So then, from what entity did this information come, if not from God? There is only one other being to consider, and that being's name is Satan.

Satan does not know everything like God does. But he does know plenty. He is around, and he is looking for people to destroy. That is what Satan does, that is who he is, the Destroyer, and he will use any tool at his disposal. He has no scruples about exploiting and deceiving the crushed heart of a grieving mother. In fact, he delights to do so.

> "Whether the phenomena are evidences of a clever trickster, demonic activity, or the staid and serious pronouncement of the sci-

entific community, the Bible calls all of it an abomination. Deuteronomy 18:9-14 says,

*When you enter the land which the Lord your God gives you, you shall not learn to imitate the detestable things of those nations. There shall not be found among you anyone who makes his son or his daughter pass through the fire, one who uses divination, one who practices witchcraft, or one who interprets omens, or a sorcerer, or one who casts a spell, or **a medium, or a spiritist, or one who calls up the dead.** For whoever does these things is detestable to the LORD; and because of these detestable things the LORD your God will drive them out before you. You shall be blameless before the LORD your God. For those nations, which you shall dispossess, listen to those who practice witchcraft and to diviners, but as for you, the LORD your God has not allowed you to do so.* (emphasis added)

"If the Old Testament saints were commanded not to seek mediums, spiritists, and the like, it's even more emphatic that clairvoyance has no place in the life of a Christian. A Christian has a personal relationship with the Father through the Lord Jesus Christ, is indwelt by the Holy Spirit, and can read and discern the mind of God in the Holy Scriptures."

John MacArthur, Grace to You:
https://www.gty.org/library/questions/QA208/does-the-bible-take-a-position-on-clairvoyance-and-parapsychology

I understand you just want confirmation your child is OK. You would give almost anything to have five more minutes with him. Your heart is hurting, and you do not know how you can bear never hearing his voice again. You know of people who have gone to a medium and nothing bad seemed to happen afterwards. But ignoring the explicit command of God is never a good idea.

Please, *do not do it!*

36 LOOKING FORWARD

It would be easy to spend all my time preoccupied with the past. The way it was. Looking at, no examining, old photographs. Studying, not just the image of our son, but the background, too. Scrutinizing the everyday scenery that has changed little but is so totally different now. Mining for the what-ifs casually arranged behind the smiling faces. Little things that might have influenced the outcome. Searching the careless backdrop of the ordinary in the pictures of what our lives used to be with Hans in it. Trying to figure out what happened.

Watching videos of Hans, listening to his voice on the answering machine, replaying old memories in my mind, smelling his clothes, touching his belongings, imagining his presence. Allowing myself to sit motionless in the ashes of missing him until I cannot function, and the cobwebs of longing choke the life out of my heart. Truly, this is what I would like to do all day long. It would be easy. But, of course, I cannot do that. There are other people to live for. New memories to make. Work to do.

Yes, I can understand how people get lost in that old slough called Despond. I understand why they become stagnant, disoriented and aimless, sometimes for the rest of their lives. I understand this. And sometimes that frightens me.

But Hans is with the Lord. And I am still here. Hans was taken for a good reason. And I am still here for a good reason. God would not allow this much pain, would not have taken Hans, unless He had a very, very, very good reason. I trust Him for this. I do not need to know the reason. Really. And, as precious as the past was, and as sweet as the memories are, it is over. Over.

So, here are the facts: Today, right this minute, the actual living Hans is not back there in the past. He is not here with me in my present except in my memories. Hans is presently very much alive, though far, far away beyond the stars, with the Lord in His beautiful, happy Heaven where I will also be someday. Hans is in my future.

Reality demands that I accept the facts as they are. It is a matter of discipline to remind myself of those facts, to believe them, and to live them with love, purpose, and praise for my Father in Heaven who loves me, and in whose presence Hans now is.

~~~

The best remedy for affliction, is sweet submission to God's providence. What can't be cured, must be endured!

<div align="right">CHARLES SPURGEON</div>

If you're going through hell, keep going.

<div align="right">WINSTON CHURCHILL</div>

37 THINGS ARE NOT WHAT THEY SEEM

One thing bereaved parents would like others to know is this: even though they may seem pretty together and functional, even though they smile, though perhaps not very brightly and not for very long; even though it seems like they are moving on with life, there are many, many things going on inside them you cannot know about. Things you cannot see, things that are not possible for you to notice.

For instance, a simple drive into town for groceries can be an emotionally exhausting experience which churns up a lifetime of memories. You have no way of knowing that, for me, almost every street in the entire city has some sort of memory associated with it. This is comforting, yes, but painful, too. You see me looking out the window at passing cars and buildings. But actually, I am looking for Hans's car or hoping to see him coming out of a store. Going into Fairbanks for the day is an emotional workout for me.

Imagine, if you will, you are with me in the car and we are spending the day shopping and running errands. What you see and what I see as we drive around town are two very different things. We are looking at the same scenery, but we are not seeing the same things.

We pull up to the Safeway gas station and you see pump No. 1 is available so you stop the car at the pump and hop out to pump the gas. I, on the other hand, have my gaze fixed on pump No. 2 right in front of us and my heart begins to hurt. Pump No. 2 is where Hans gassed up his car exactly 3 hours and 15 minutes before the crash. I know this because I found the receipt in his jacket pocket: 1/11/16; 02:48:54 p.m.; 8.126 gal. Total sale: $22.18. I imagine him there at pump No. 2 wearing his black and white jacket and sunglasses, so handsome, happily pumping gas, not knowing he had a little over three hours to live.

I turn away from pump No. 2 and look straight ahead. You would see a fast-food joint, a traffic light, and a couple of scrawny birch trees. But I see something else. Between the Carl's Jr. sign and the Fred Meyer entrance sign, beyond the scrawny birch trees and the traffic light, I see a funeral home, the very one where I last saw my son's face.

I shift my eyes to the left. You would see a hotel. I see a hotel, too, one that I know has a very nice restaurant upstairs. I know this because our family has eaten there many times. In fact, Manfred and Hans ate breakfast there often while working on their last house of the season a few months before Hans left us. I know exactly which table they sat at and now, when we eat there, I cannot seem to take my eyes off this table. I also see the large table in the center of the restaurant, the one with six chairs, where we ate so many meals together as a family. We no longer require the large table for six people. Other families sit there now.

But back to the gas station and the shopping trip. I force my eyes to look beyond pump No. 2 to the Safeway store itself. You see a grocery store. I see the parking lot in front of it where Manfred and Hans used to sit drinking iced tea on their lunch breaks. This is the parking lot from which they always called me before heading home, to ask if I needed anything from the store.

I swivel my head a complete one hundred eighty degrees. You see another grocery store. I see through the walls of it into the toy department where Manfred and I used to let the children blow off steam before buckling them back into the old station wagon for the trip home. In those days, they had a T.V. and a few little chairs in the toy department and that is where I would sit nursing the current infant and where I would change the current infant's diaper behind that rack of clothes where the boys' clothing department adjoins the toy department. Hans bought a lot of caps for his toy guns here.

Finally, we leave the gas station. We are hungry and decide on pizza, and pizza means Geraldo's over on College Road. We find a seat and we hear the usual Italian restaurant tunes in the background: Frank Sinatra, Dean Martin, Mel Torme, etc. However, right after ordering a large Magna Carne pizza, my ears pick up on a song I have never heard before. It is Josh Groban's, "To Where You Are."

There is no escape. We have already ordered. I try not to listen too closely and start reciting Social Security and bank account numbers in my head to distract myself. It is a beautiful song inviting me to lose myself in tears; I force myself to think about the dessert menu instead. Then, up next is Nat King Cole singing, "Smile." The heaviness deepens.

Blinking swiftly, I look around for Hans. My eyes fasten onto an empty table ten feet away. Our table. I remember last year, the waitress stepping on Hans's foot three times as she served us, maybe because she was new or maybe to get his attention because Hans was looking extra devastating that day.

Why do Italian restaurants play such gut-wrenching music? Is this a marketing ploy? Do sad people eat more pizza? I am doing pretty well with the SSN's, managing not to drop a single tear though I am hungry, tired of fighting it, and ready to go home and just sit in a chair. I try not to look around too much because everywhere I see the empty tables where Hans once sat. The pizza finally arrives, my panic subsides, we eat and get out of there.

Onward to the Co-Op Market to get something to drink. This is where Hans liked to shop for snacks and personal grooming products. Hans was big on personal grooming products. On the way, we pass a closed up mini-mall. You see a dilapidated vacant building. I see the old model store where we bought so many Christmas presents for Hans during the heyday of his model building career.

We leave there and the ordeal is nearly finished. We cruise up Airport Way. You see the Two Dice Pawn Shop, Coin King, and a Napa Store. But I see the place where Hans found us a generator when ours was history and we couldn't afford a new one. I see the laundromat where I washed his baby clothes and where he later pushed his little brothers around in laundry baskets on wheels when he was a boy. I see where he bought parts for our vehicles as a grown-up man.

I am exhausted. I look around Fairbanks at peoples' faces. Some of them look like they are hurting. I wonder what *they* are seeing.

38 LETTER TO A FRIEND

Rejoice with them that do rejoice,
and weep with them that weep. Romans 12:15

One thing that ministered to me the most after Hans left us was the genuine sorrow people shared with us. It is a sweet joy when folks are brave enough to let me know Hans mattered to them, too. Thank you for saying his name out loud.

I wrote the following letter in response to a friend who called to express her sorrow about Hans:

Hi _____,

Manfred mentioned he stopped by your place, and you have been on my mind ever since. This is very hard for all of us that knew and loved Hans; I am honored by your tears. Please tell your boys that Hans thought a great deal of them. He often said he wished there were more boys like yours out there.

I want you to know that, while our hearts are so very, very heavy, we do not grieve as those who have no hope. Tomorrow is Easter Sunday and all I can think about is that someday, maybe soon, Hans will come up out of that hole where we planted him, and he will be physically raised with a brand new, unbroken, perfect body that can never die. These are the facts of the resurrection. I know you know this. But I also want you to know that I have found Jesus can be trusted to do what he says he will do. I believe what He said.

Here are the facts—God's Word, the Bible, is very clear: To be absent from the body is to be present with the Lord. The moment life went out of Hans's body, he was taken immediately into the presence of God—no waiting, no further payment or cleansing required. That is because Jesus paid it all and it is finished.

When the Lord Jesus returns, he will bring Hans with him. Hans is not dead. He is very much alive and having a wonderful, beautiful time right this very minute. We will see him again and we know exactly where he is. He has left our home and gone on ahead to his eternal home. We know this because Hans believed what God says about sin and how to be saved from it.

This is not the vague hope of a grieving mother: ("I *hope* he's in heaven.") No, this is a *sure* hope—a joyful certainty: *"I know he's in heaven!"* Hans is safe. He is where no one can hurt him. I do not need to worry about him. January 11, 2016 was the best day of Hans's life. I pray you know these things with the same certainty and that it brings you peace. — Kim

~~~

God's Providence not only extends to mankind in general, and to the beasts of the field, and the birds of the air, and the innumerable fish in the sea—but also to every atom of matter in the universe!

CHARLES SPURGEON

It [the resurrection] proved him to be the Son of God, inasmuch as it authenticated all his claims 'But now is Christ risen from the dead, and become the first-fruits of them that slept.' (1 Corinthians 15:20) Therefore, the Bible is true from Genesis to Revelation.

HODGE

39 THE CRUX OF THE MATTER

Without the Resurrection, if Jesus Christ did not rise bodily from the dead, then our departed son is also dead, just dead, and the whole churchy Bible thing is a bogus fabrication. Without a living Jesus, Hans is *gone. Forever.*

> "The bodily resurrection of Jesus Christ from the dead is the crowning proof of Christianity. Everything else that was said or done by Christ and the apostles is secondary in importance to the resurrection. If the resurrection did not take place, then Christianity is a false religion. If it did take place, then Christ is God and the Christian faith is absolute truth."
>
> Henry M. Morris, Ph.D.
> The Resurrection of Christ—The Best-Proved Fact in History
> https://www.icr.org/ChristResurrection/

If Jesus is not alive, then I have believed a lie and will never see our Hans again. Without a risen Savior, there is no Heaven, no reunion, no peace, no answers, no forgiveness, no rewards for good and no justice dispensed for evil. In fact, if God the Son is not Who He says He is, then there *is* no evil; all those horrible things we blame God for are just the natural behaviors of the human animal.

Without the living God, I have no purpose, no Truth, no hope, no Hans. I simply could not live with that.

40 ANGRY AT GOD

Anger. We have all experienced it. Sometimes it is a burning, churning, table-pounding rage. At other times, it is more of a low-grade infection that burrows deep into the heart. It simmers on the back burner of the mind, giving off an unpleasant aroma, occasionally boiling over and making an unsightly mess. For a variety of reasons, anger at the Almighty is not uncommon among parents dealing with child loss.

Some have lost children because of the wickedness of others. A heartbreaking number of young people, overwhelmed with pain, have ended their own life. There are children who endured years of sickness and suffering, and there are those who left us quickly with no warning. Some made terrible, irreversible mistakes and got into situations they could not get out of.

And now they are gone.

No matter how your child died, there will probably come a time when you just want it to make sense. Some are OK with waiting until eternity to see the big picture. But many want to know *now* what God had in mind by allowing this. Understandably, they are distraught. They are in pain; they are angry, and they are demanding to know *Why?*

Tragically, some decide that any answer God might come up with would simply not be good enough. In their bleeding, battered heart, they shake their fist at the sky and pronounce God's plan unacceptable. Many are mad at Someone they do not even believe exists. Or, if He exists, He is not the kind of god they want to believe in. They feel they could do a better job of things. *I'll decide which god is right for me. I don't need a god who lets bad things happen to me. If there must be a god, I'll be my own god.* They rage at Him because they do not know Him.

There is neither logic nor peace in grief that is encumbered with unbelief. Anger at God just makes it worse.

One does not need to look far before encountering unspeakable evil in this world, and anger is the right and natural response to it. As I write this, perversions of every sort are being perpetrated, recorded, and posted on the very internet I use to share the Good News of Jesus Christ. Young girls are being sold into slavery for the twisted pleasures of despicable men. Thievery is commonplace. Deception proliferates. Darkness seems to rule.

In our limited capacity to understand the ways of God, we think: *How can God possibly redeem the brutal, vicious crimes committed daily against honest men, helpless children and defenseless women? These horrors cannot be undone. There is no conceivable good that can be expected to make up for it.* And then, we begin to accuse Him:

How could you let this happen?
What did I do to deserve this terrible loss?
Where were you, God?
I don't think you know what you are doing, God.
There is no God. If there is, I am mad as ___ at Him.
It's not fair!

This kind of anger can be annihilating. It will wreck your health, your relationships, and what is left of your broken heart. It will ferment and grow and spill out all over your life. In fact, it can crush you. Anger piled on top of grief is too heavy a burden to bear. Anger at God (or at anyone, including ourselves) makes grief much more complicated.

Anger is certainly an appropriate response to evil. However, the pain of bereavement can make us especially vulnerable to protracted or misplaced anger. I am convinced that staying too long in a place of seething outrage is counterproductive and makes the pain of child loss worse by several orders of magnitude for the grieving parent and for those around them. Unchecked anger hands the victory over to evil.

There is nothing wrong with being angry about the evil that may have been perpetrated against your child. God is angry about it, too. But we need to be careful about how and where we direct this anger.

Anger can be harnessed and transformed into a productive force for good. I have seen parents who have taken the pain of child loss and used it as an impetus for change in the world. Rather than stewing in a boiling pot of bitterness, they are reaching out, even while in the thick storm of grieving, to help others, to raise awareness, to instruct and to comfort. They start campaigns and found organizations. They establish scholarships, build parks, and teach kids to swim. Parents like this amaze me, and I salute them. Their efforts enrich the rest of us. Their loss becomes gain for the many lives they touch. Their departed child impacts the world in a beautiful and productive way, maybe even more than if they had not died.

So, what we do with this anger is key. We need to take care not to indulge in anger to the point where it festers into a simmering spirit of bitterness that permeates the soul and infects our relationships. When we demand to exercise our "right" to be angry, we feed the anger by continuing to focus on the circumstances of our loss. This makes the anger grow and spread into every area of our life. We fiercely grip our anger and, with hot, furious tears, turn our face away from God. Anger takes over. The heart turns to stone. Evil wins.

Are you angry at God because you are suffering, or your child has suffered, and God does not seem to care? Are you angry because you have been robbed of your only child and God did not intervene? Are you angry because there is no justice: the murderer goes free, the drug pusher goes unpunished, life goes on and your child is still dead? Are you angry because God does not put a stop to the whole appalling mess?

Here is good news for you: *He will.* God is in control and, in His perfect timing, when the last sinner has been added to His church, He will make everything right. The worst ugliness that man can dish out to man will be rectified. There will be justice. The apparent delay in no way negates the fact that God is love. He loves you and He loves your child. He loves justice and mercy because He *is* Justice and Mercy. No one gets away with anything, and it is sobering to consider the torment that awaits the perpetrators of these heinous acts. Unless they turn to God for forgiveness through the blood of Jesus, God's own crucified and risen son, they will *pay. Forever.*

God's justice is thorough, and it is eternal. I do not mean that God will merely make it all better. No, it will be infinitely more expansive than that. The fulfillment of His ultimate plan will be so far beyond the word "*right*"—well, there are no words in any language to express it.

Anger is destructive. It is a nasty weapon in the Destroyer's arsenal. How is it working for you? Does it not make you unbelievably tired? Wouldn't you like to lay it down and walk away? Wouldn't you like to replace it with something more productive? Wouldn't you like to rest?

There is relief to be had from the smothering heaviness of anger. Take it all to your Father in Heaven—all of it. Tell Him the whole rotting mess and ask Him to take it from you. Ask Him to lift it from your weary shoulders so you can grieve with joy and peace rather than ugly bitterness. Then give it up and walk away. By doing so, you are not walking away from your child. You are walking away from the anger. You are walking toward peace.

If you do not know Jesus, ask Him to reveal Himself to you. He is real, He is there, and He is able to meet you and save you right where you are.

~~~

Believing that God rules all, that He governs wisely, that He brings good out of evil, the believer is enabled calmly to meet each trial as it comes. He can in the spirit of true resignation pray, "Send me what you will, my God–so long as it comes from You! A bad portion never came from Your table to any of Your redeemed children."

C.H. Spurgeon

Joni Eareckson Tada on Doubting God's Goodness:

"Although so many so-called Christian therapists will try to convince you that it's okay to lay it all out and vent your anger against God full force. Some will even tell you that you need to forgive God... friend that is the wrong advice. Never cast aspersions on His character; never talk behind His back; never sow seeds of discord about Him among others—not only does it dishonor the Lord, but it'll definitely make things worse for you... much worse."

"... at the first hint of fear or doubt or anger I rehearsed in my mind everything I had ever learned about His sovereignty: God is good, He always has my best interests at heart; He is kind and merciful and He doesn't take His hands off the wheel of my life for a nanosecond. He's in control and He's got reasons for allowing this."

"I had to recognize my limited ability to understand God's ways. Look, like you I have a finite and very fallen mind that is simply incapable of comprehending God's dealings with man. I had to recognize I'm not responsible for figuring out God; only for knowing, trusting and pleasing Him."

"Finally, when tempted to be angry at God, you don't need to settle for being a cold stoic or hot-headed blasphemer. God has opened the door for you to lament, to bring to Him your doubts and questions, wisely, honestly, and in humility. He bends His ear to His suffering people—and He's waiting to hear from you today."

JONI EARECKSON TADA
Angry at God (excerpts, used with permission)
© Joni and Friends www.joniandfriends.org

41 EMPTY STALLS, EMPTY BEDS

Most of our animals were acquired when our children were young. Our oldest animal, a goat (The Old Lady), died at the ripe old age of eleven just a few months after Hans left us. She was one of our original breeding stock and was sensible and reliable as a goat can be. But one day the old gal just could not get up anymore. She was healthy, still enjoyed chewing her way through a day in the sunshine, but she was done, and she let us know it. Just a goat, but another break with The Way Things Used to Be.

A few months later our buck, whom we never did name, and on whom the whole operation depended, turned up dead in his pen one crisp fall morning with no explanation. Just old and unwilling to face another winter, I guess. So, Rosebud (The Old Lady's daughter—sleek, spunky, and psychologically unbalanced), is the only resident ruminant on the place now. And that is fine with her—she likes the extra attention. However, for some odd reason, she did not conceive this season. We are blaming the old buck, though I cannot believe a male goat ever loses his vigor no matter how old he is.

Then the rabbits started dying, one by one. I had forgotten that when we brought them home, we were still driving the old Custom Cruiser station wagon, which was our primary vehicle when the children were growing up. Hans was very attached to "The Cruiser" and planned on restoring it someday. He made a good start on the rust repair some years ago, but then moved on to other things. Sometimes I look through its clouded windows at the vacant plush maroon seats. There is junk in it from that last trip to town still on the floor, and the seat belts are flung here and there as if they were just unbuckled by sticky little hands.

We lost some chickens over the winter, not unusual but a loss just the same. And our regular local moose performed a severe and unwelcome pruning job on my roses, including the ones I planted at Hans's resting place. The cat walked off one day and never came back. And our dog, (our daughter's dog) has a few gray hairs and is moving a little slower. I would rather not lose the dog any time soon.

Then our daughter moved out—not far, just down the highway—but now there are two empty beds in the house instead of one. Not a problem, just emptiness where sweet treasure used to sleep.

So, we are experiencing some changes right now. Some big, some smaller, all under the complete control of our loving Lord. I sense that one season of life is ending, and another is beginning. I have never liked change, especially major ones. Change can be unsettling and often inconvenient. But after giving Hans back to the Lord, most changes barely register on my Richter scale. I do not know what the Lord has planned for us. We rest in knowing He is God, and that He knows what He is doing.

I began this journey without knowing all the twists and turns it may involve. But my Captain knows all. I do not need to fret or peer over His shoulder to make sure He is on the right course. I am just along for the ride wherever He takes me. I trust the Captain because I know Him. And He knows me. This is peace.

> *Although the fig tree shall not blossom,*
> *neither shall fruit be in the vines; the labour of the*
> *olive shall fail, and the fields shall yield no meat;*
> *the flock shall be cut off from the fold, and there*
> *shall be no herd in the stalls: Yet I will rejoice in the*
> *LORD, I will joy in the God of my salvation.*
> *Habakkuk 3:17-18*

42 WHAT IS THIS THING CALLED FAITH?

Now faith is the substance of things hoped for, the evidence of things not seen. Hebrews 11:1

Since Hans went home to be with the Lord on 1/11/16, whenever I see the numbers 1 and 11 together, it catches my eye. For me, they are numbers that are hard to forget.

So, one morning in May, at the start of our second Spring without Hans, I was thinking on Hebrews 11:1 as I finished my tea. Later that day, I was organizing a shelf of Hans's old high school stuff, deciding which of his textbooks our youngest son would use the following fall for his senior year. From between the pages of grammar, government, and chemistry books, scraps of memories on college-ruled notebook paper slipped through my fingers and drifted silently to the floor.

I picked up one of the Bible study workbooks Hans used for his junior year and started flipping through it, smiling at his easily recognized, hurry-up handwriting. The book fell open to lesson thirty-five: *The Life of Faith, Part One*. There, at the top of page one hundred twenty-three, was the question: *What is Faith?* And then Hans's answer: *the evidence of things not seen*. There was space available to expand on the answer, but he added nothing profound or original. Hans was definitely a get-to-the-point and get-it-done kind of guy.

Then, down the page to question six: *What two things should you keep in mind in order to help you endure the afflictions of this life?* Hans's answer: (a) r*emember God's past blessings,* and (b) *keep in mind the rewards you have coming.*

I take these words, Hans's answers to question six, (a) and (b) above, as counsel straight from Heaven. They are often the very words I need to say to myself to get through difficult moments. To have it in Hans's own handwriting is a treasure.

Back up to question two: *What makes faith great?* Hans's answer: *Its object.* Which brings me to my point: What is Faith?

I am not a theologian. I am just an average mom with a very bruised heart. Since the crash, my memory is shot, I find it difficult to make conversation, and my word-finding ability has declined considerably. Therefore, I will not get technical here. But I *will* give you what I know and understand faith to be. So here we go.

What faith is not...

Faith is not confidence in one's self, one's merit, ability, religion or support group. Faith placed in anything other than the person and work of The Lord Jesus Christ will not suffice. I could fool myself into a state of "peace and safety" by inventing nice, comforting theories and adopting them as my personal dogma, but that would be self-deceptive idolatry, an ineffectual fabrication, and an abomination to God. Faith is not something I muster up as needed. It is not an attitude or a way of thinking, though faith will certainly *affect* my attitude and thinking.

Faith is not wishful thinking or a vague sense that everything will work out for the best because "I have faith." Faith in what? In myself? In my power to determine my destiny? Faith in my friends, my husband, my children, my pastor, priest, rabbi, education, will, strength, credentials, credit cards, political connections, the harmony of the universe? None of these will get me far.

Let me tell you something. When you stand next to a hole in the ground into which they are about to lower your son, NONE of those things will do the job. When they are throwing shovels-full of dirt on your heart, when clods of frozen earth splatter onto the box that contains your son, you need the real deal. You need something powerful, more powerful than the blinding pain sucking the marrow from your bones. More powerful than breathless lungs and a motionless heart. More powerful than cold, irreversible, unmerciful, soul-hammering, lifelessness. You need faith—real, trusting, unshakeable Faith. You need substance, evidence, hope. You need something, Someone, to keep you breathing. *You need God.* Nothing and no one else are big enough.

What faith is:

Faith is believing what God has said. Faith must have as its object something bigger than self. Bigger than anyone or anything. Faith must be in something *bigger than death*. There is no point in having a lot of faith in something little.

Apparently, there are some who believe they can do Death of a Child without God, without faith, and keep functioning. I am not one of them. I would not want to, even if I could. I would not, could not bear purposeless, on top of hopeless, on top of Godless, on top of My Son Is Dead. No. Way. I could never, ever scratch together enough faith to live without Faith. And neither, if you are honest, can you.

*An important note: An unregenerate person—one who has not been born again from above—cannot know true believing faith as presented in God's Word, the Bible. However, if you honestly desire to grasp the substance of a living, saving hope-filled faith and to personally *know* the only One who, based on evidence of things seen and unseen, can deliver you from sin, death, heartbreak and hopelessness, then do this: Ask Jesus to reveal Himself to you. Lay aside your sin, your self, and all the junk that you know is not working for you and come to Him just as you are. He is waiting and able to transform you, to live inside of you and to save you from the penalty and power of sin forever. Only by believing and trusting in Him can the concept of true faith, of *sure* hope, become real to you.

For whosoever shall call upon the name of the Lord shall be saved. Romans 10:13

43 THOUGHTS ON PSALM 105:1-5

O give thanks unto the LORD; call upon his name:
make known his deeds among the people.

Thank you, Lord, that you *are*. Thank you I can call on your name and you hear me. *Me!* Thank you I have the freedom to tell people about your marvelous deeds. Thank you for all you do for us that love you and even for those who despise you. Thank you for saving me from sin and death by sending your Son, Jesus, to die in my place.

2. Sing unto him, sing psalms unto him: talk ye of
all his wondrous works.

Everything you do is wonderful—even those things I do not understand. Especially those things. By your power, you hold all things together: the water I drink, the ground I stand on, the atmosphere I breathe, the granite stone with our son's name carved into it, the particles within the atoms of my bruised and hurting heart. You alone hold the universe together by the power of your might, by the force of your will, by the strength of your love.

3. Glory ye in his holy name: let the heart of them
rejoice that seek the LORD.

Your name is holy and pure. No other name under Heaven has the power to save a sinner or to raise the dead. Someday every knee will bow, and every tongue will confess that you are Lord. You are my Savior. Every day I seek to be near you, and I rejoice you are always with me.

4. Seek the LORD, and his strength:
seek his face evermore.

I need your strength. When I am weak, you are strong, and able to carry me where I need to go. You make me what I need to be. Keep me close or I am nothing. I cannot wait to see your face.

5. Remember his marvellous works
that he hath done; his wonders, and the
judgments of his mouth;

Let me never, ever forget what I am without you. Everything you do is wonderful and right. Everything.

44 FIRST ANNIVERSARY

The days and weeks leading up to The Day which forever marks the death of a loved one can be difficult. For some, the anticipation is far worse than the actual day, with the first anniversary usually being the hardest (but not always). Many parents fear the one-year anniversary day will be as horrendous as the original loss day. Thankfully, it usually is not.

For me, the pain of One Year Day was minor compared to the actual day of Hans's departure and the weeks that followed. The first anniversary was not much worse than any other day (they all hurt) except I did a lot more clock watching as the time of the crash approached and I recalled what each of us was doing during those final hours and minutes of our Old Life.

We did not plan anything, just did regular life & paused whenever anyone remembered something and felt like talking. We said little about it; we all knew we were remembering in our own way. The following day (Hans's birthday) was a little more difficult for me and the week that followed churned up some old cortisol left over from the year before and threw it up on my shore. But it was manageable.

I could tell some folks did not know what to expect on "D Day" as one person put it (yes, really). I could see it in their eyes. They seemed kind of nervous. Maybe they were relieved I did not fall apart in their presence; or maybe they were disappointed I did not act as they anticipated. Some dear ones remembered with me; or sent a card with genuine feelings, written in their own handwriting on the inside of the card, opposite the pretty printed sentiment. A few said Hans's name; most did not.

I suppose I could have shared with them that grieving vigorously, constructively, biblically, and thoroughly (and, except for the Lord, mostly alone) those first months after the crash, helped to later modulate the expected anniversary day emotional upheaval. I did much of the hard grief work the year before, but how could anyone know that? So, I kept it fairly together on One Year Day.

Sometimes flagrant self-control is viewed as commendable and inspiring. Sometimes it is frowned upon as being fake. Nevertheless, I asked the Lord for grace to maintain composure for The Day, for my sake and for the sake of those near me. Thankfully, He graciously granted my plea, and it made for an atmosphere of peace and of quiet reminiscing as I floated carefully through the day. Grief did not dominate, Hans was remembered; I pray God was honored.

Temporary composure notwithstanding, I am still not "over it." Those crushing I-cannot-believe-he-is-gone moments still come. But, more often, grief has diminished to more of a dull ache that I drag around rather than a terrifying train wreck kind of feeling that knocks me over. I have come to see those horrible grief bursts for what they are: sometimes it is just me missing my boy and that's OK. But other times (more rarely, now) it is a desperate grasping and clutching to make him *be* here, to make him come back. That's *not* OK, and not productive. I learned early on, if I lose it too much I just do not feel well, and I can easily become a total drag for the rest of the family. And Hans would want me to be happy. I know this because he used to often check to make sure that I was.

So, on anniversaries, and on just regular days, I repeat the facts to myself: On January 11, 2016, Hans was taken up to Glory and received into the company of just men made perfect. This is good news, the best news. Hans is with the Lord, which is far better for him. Hans is happy and safe, and I will see him again—maybe soon, if Jesus returns while I am still scratching around on these ten acres.

Ask the Lord to help you not to fear that One Year Day. Yes, the pain can be fierce, and the missing is heavy, but you have already been through the worst of it. Compared to the day your precious child left for Heaven, the day the earth moved, and your heart was fractured to its core... well, the rest of it is aftershocks. And since aftershocks can do a lot of damage, too, make sure your heart and mind are resting on a solid Foundation. It is the first step in rebuilding.

~~~

The work of grace, though it is above nature, is not against it. The man who tells me not to weep at the grave insults me, mocks me, and wishes to degrade me! Tears are the silent, pure, sincere testimony of my heart to the excellence of the gift He gave in mercy; and in mercy, no doubt, as well as judgment, He has recalled. But though we mourn, we must not murmur. We may sorrow, but not with the passionate and uncontrolled grief of the heathen who have no hope. Our sorrow may flow as deep as we like but noiseless and still, in the channels of submission.

<div align="right">JOHN ANGELL JAMES (1785-1859)</div>

How shall I sing the Lord's song in a strange land? For I am brought into a strange, weary land of loneliness and sorrow. I am a captive to grief, and the light of my life has been suddenly quenched in darkness. Yet there is a song to be sung. Mercy has outrun misery. Divine love has pierced the gloom of an unspeakable sorrow with a ray of celestial glory. The anguished cry of a stricken heart has been hushed by the sweet compassion of a comforting God! Praise the Lord! Praise the Lord, O my soul! It is the Lord's song... He will help me to sing it.

<div align="right">SUSANNAH SPURGEON</div>

45 CHILD LOSS: WHY WE ARE UNCOMFORTABLE

When someone is widowed after decades of marriage, or loses an elderly parent, perhaps after a long decline in health, we can usually empathize because these deaths follow the typical order of life; the loss, though painful, is not unusual. Often we can anticipate the end of life well in advance, and though the grief of loved ones left behind is real and deep, we seem to be less apprehensive when we encounter someone grieving a parent or older person because the death was expected; losses like this will happen to all of us.

But child loss, being an out-of-order death, is different. It is so different that most people who have not been through it may struggle with how to interact with someone who has. When encountering a grieving parent in a social situation, the non-bereaved may feel awkward or uncomfortable. Why is this? It is because there is no way to become *comfortable* with child loss.

Sometimes the discomfort springs from selfishness, insensitivity, or rudeness. The bereaved become an elephant in a room full of oblivious "Life is Good" T-shirt wearers, who do not want their parade rained on. Not having ever suffered (yet), they have little experience to draw from and would prefer not to have to deal with your emotional baggage right now.

But I think most often the problem is fear. The non-bereaved are on unfamiliar ground. And it is scary. *What do I do? What do I say? Better to avoid this person than risk making a mess of things.*

Before our loss, when in the presence of a bereaved mother who started talking about her departed child, I would get uncomfortable, too. All would be fine if the conversation was unrelated to her dead child, but as soon as *It* came up, I would instantly feel anxious. I was not irritated because she was spoiling my fun or ruining a good day for me or demanding attention. I was uncomfortable because of the pity I felt for her, which embarrassed me on her behalf. No one wants to be the object of pity.

And I worried I might not have an easy fix for her. I believed I should be able to wave my magic tongue and make her feel all better somehow but, like a dope, I left my handy toolbox full of helpful platitudes at home that day. I drew a blank when brought face to face with the grown-up world of Hardship and sensed my imaginary reputation as a wise and helpful counselor was in imminent jeopardy. The truth is, I felt incompetent.

I could not feel genuine compassion for her because I had not yet experienced a comparable loss—and because I was focused on my own performance. Though I fooled myself into thinking so, it was not compassion I felt for this woman. It was pure pity for her continued state of pain, which made her attempts at making people know or remember her son seem pathetic to me. To the pre-loss me, she seemed inappropriately stuck in the past (despite her smile) or maybe even mentally and emotionally damaged because of the trauma she had gone through. To my uninitiated eyes, she looked incredibly strong and pitifully weak all at the same time. And it made me uncomfortable.

And I was afraid. I sensed danger and thought, *What if she opens up and I don't have any answers for her? What if she, gulp, cries? What if she loses control and I can't help her get back to normal? What if I fail to comfort her? Maybe she needs professional help. What if I say something wrong? What if I make it worse? How bad might it get?*

What I know now is that this woman was simply sharing what was on her mind—her gone-too-soon child. She was missing her baby and needed to express that. She needed to hear his name spoken out loud. That's all. No pathology, no selfish appropriation of available compassion. No attention seeking. Just a mom missing her child.

I am selective about who I talk to about our loss because I don't want people to look at me with pity the way I looked at her. That's pride, without a doubt. And in social settings, as a textbook introvert who prefers to operate in the background, I realize that speaking about a child that has died does in fact draw attention. How could it not? I must be careful to remember there are others present who might be hurting as much or more than I. Child loss is not the only sorrow. It may be someone else's turn to be comforted or encouraged right now.

Even if the world forgets our children (and it will), we will not. And, thankfully, our Father in Heaven remembers every single moment of their lives. Though it is a strong temptation, I don't have to bring Hans up in *every* conversation in order to keep his memory alive. I have more than a memory. I have a living son. True, he lives very far away, but he is as close to me as the love of my Savior.

So, to those who desire to reach out to a hurting friend who has suffered the loss of a child, I say, Be uncomfortable. Don't fight it because *there is no way to become comfortable with child loss*. Don't be afraid. Share a memory of or something you admired about the departed one. If your tears are genuine, let them fall. They are a sweet blessing to a hurting heart.

Unless your motive is morbid curiosity or you are fishing for some sort of inside story; unless your interest is merely that of a spectator, or your aim is to wound, you cannot possibly make child loss worse than it already is. And it's OK to be uncomfortable.

~~~

"I wish everyone knew about E. I am most uncomfortable in places where I know there is no one there who knew she existed."

E's MOM

46 ON PRAYER

A common question that comes up among bereaved parents has to do with prayer. Specifically, the parent wants to know why, after begging God for the life of her child, the child died anyway. Or perhaps the child himself prayed to get well or a whole prayer chain of people prayed and still the child died. They want to know: *Why didn't God answer my prayer? Wasn't my prayer good enough? Am I not good enough? Is God punishing me? Is He even there?*

Why Didn't God Answer My Prayer?

The fact is, for the believer in the one true and living God, every prayer is answered. His answer may be yes, no, or not yet. He may delay answering or grant it in a way that is totally unexpected or even unwelcome. For instance, our family often prays for safety. Safety on the highway, safety on the job, safety in the woods, etc. And at the end of the day, when the person we prayed for walks through the door, we think, *God has answered our prayer. He has given us what we asked for.*

But what if the person we prayed for gets injured or, even worse, does not come home at all? If we did not receive what we asked for, does that mean God did not answer our prayer? No, of course not. It just means God has another plan. A better plan, though it may not look better to us at all.

When Hans went to the highway for the last time, we did not pray for his safety. He planned on being gone maybe five minutes to test some work he just did on the engine. What could happen in five minutes? So, did the crash happen because we neglected to pray this one time? Were all those other times we prayed for his safety just a waste of time? Hans crashed his car, was fatally injured, and died within minutes. How can this possibly be an answer to *any* of our prayers? Where were health and safety that night for Hans? Where was this God who answers prayer?

God was right there with my boy. God *did* answer our prayers. Hans was instantly safe with the Father the moment he left his battered body in the car. What outcome could be better *for Hans?*

The problem is with words like safety, healing, recovery, and so on. We have our own little definitions for these words. When we take the eternal view of things, health and safety may mean something entirely different from what we suppose they should mean. Another problem is that we expect an answer from God that will cause us the least amount of discomfort. We do not truly want what is best for everyone the way God does. We are selfish. We do not want to suffer. We want to be happy and pain free—all the time, if possible. We often pray amiss. Sometimes, we are not actually praying but worrying out loud, trying to lay out all the possibilities in case God needs help in selecting a course of action.

Satan delights when we question God's power and promises, and is ready to whisper a suggestion of doubt as we begin to pray a promise. *Go ahead, pray the promise and see where it gets you.* Or maybe he might accuse us as we pray, bringing up past events, sins or false guilt, which can hinder our prayer and make it seem as if God is reneging on the promise. A swift cry to the Lord for help at such times will fill us with the help we need to pray past any doubt and away from any sin, and to get up off our knees with the quiet assurance that the promise is sure.

If we truly desire for our prayers to be heard, if we genuinely want to be more like Jesus, if we long for our faith to be strengthened, we will count it all joy when trials come our way. Prayer becomes our lifeline, connecting us with the Lord who loves us. As we pray for His will to be done, we see His hand in every sorrow and we thank Him for the blessing of His comfort and strength during the storm. Our prayers become more thankful and less complaining. They become a sweet aroma to our Father in Heaven. His will becomes our joy.

I thank my God He has provided a way for me to know his will. By spending time in His Word and time in believing prayer, I can be confident that He hears me, that He will always answer in His perfect timing, and that His provision will be exactly the right thing—for all of us.

There is a limit to the doctrine of the prayer of faith. We are not to expect that God will give us everything we choose to ask for. We know that we sometimes ask, and do not receive, because we ask amiss. If we ask for that which is not promised; if we run counter to the spirit which the Lord would have us cultivate; if we ask contrary to His will, or to the decrees of His providence; if we ask merely for the gratification of our own ease, and without an eye to His glory, we must not expect that we shall receive. Yet, when we ask in faith, nothing doubting, if we receive not the precise thing asked for, we shall receive an equivalent, and more than an equivalent, for it. As one remarks, 'If the Lord does not pay in silver, He will in gold; and if He does not pay in gold, He will in diamonds.' If He does not give you precisely what you ask for, He will give you that which is tantamount to it, and that which you will greatly rejoice to receive in lieu thereof. Be then, dear reader, much in prayer, and make this evening a season of earnest intercession, but take heed what you ask.

C. H. SPURGEON

When Prayer is Hard

> *Casting all your care upon him;*
> *for he careth for you. 1 Peter 5:7*

You know you are supposed to pray, but you just can't. Not now. You want to ask Him for safety and protection for your loved ones, but you hesitate, knowing from experience the answer to that prayer might not be what you expect. Maybe it has been a long time since you have spoken to the Lord at all.

What do you say to God when you cannot find words to express your sorrow, your fears, your anger, disappointment, regret? You hurt, but there is no way to express it other than weeping, immersing yourself in the pain, and feeling the entire weight of it down into your soul. As it is often said, *there are no words.*

> *Even to day is my complaint bitter: my stroke is heavier than my groaning. Job 23:2*

When you do not know what to say to God, remember that you need not say anything. He hears and understands your groaning, and every tear is a prayer in itself.

> *I am weary with my groaning; all the night make I my bed to swim; I water my couch with my tears. Psalm 6:6*

If you are still early in your grief, maybe crying out to Him in your pain is all you can do for a while. That's OK. He knows what is in your heart and pouring it all out to Him *is* prayer.

> *Likewise the Spirit also helpeth our infirmities: for we know not what we should pray for as we ought: but the Spirit itself maketh intercession for us with groanings which cannot be uttered. Romans 8:26*

The peace God offers us when we pray does not necessarily mean an absence of pain. His peace is more of a resting in the sorrow while trusting God for the answers to questions that would otherwise torment us. Peace means to cease from striving against what God has allowed in our lives and in the lives of our children. It is giving over what we want and receiving what God has willed. It is letting go of what could have been and accepting what is. In the beginning of loss, everything in us fights against this. And so, we suffer. This is normal. Give yourself time. God is faithful. Do not fight Him. Peace will come.

Prayer is our connection to the God of peace and hope. When you cannot find the words, just get alone before Him and *hurt*. Give to Him all you are feeling. Confess whatever lurks in your heart that is unholy. Praise His name, even if you don't feel like it. Even if you do not have an ounce of honest thankfulness to offer Him, just say it: "God is good." Say it because it is true.

Do not cut yourself off from your best Friend. He loves you and is waiting to hear from you. He alone can make life a joy again.

~~~

If God has given His Son to die for us, let us beware of doubting His kindness and love in any painful providence of our daily life.

J. C. Ryle

Grief is like a sacrament to those who share it with Christ beside them. It brings them into a holier fellow-ship than they have ever known in love's unclouded days. Many homes have been saved from harshness of spirit, and sharpness of speech, from pride and coldness and heedlessness, by a sorrow which broke in upon the careless life. The tones were softer after that. There was a new gentleness in all the life. Most of us need the chastening of pain to bring out the best of our love.

J. R. Miller 1896

Before I was afflicted I went astray:
but now have I kept thy word. Psalm 119:67

47 GRIEF BRAIN? ME?

I am sitting in the third-row pew in our empty church, waiting for Wednesday evening prayer meeting to start. As the warm summer sun streams through the windows, I am enjoying the quietness of the building as I wait for the others to arrive.

Seven o'clock comes and goes. I am wondering what is keeping everyone and I think about becoming irritated—I truly appreciate punctuality. Then, slowly, I realize I must consider the possibility that, though I have arrived early for Wednesday prayer meeting, it may not be Wednesday at all. It might, in fact, be Tuesday.

How can I verify this? I do not have a cell phone. I could walk over to the library and casually check the date on one of their computers, but if it *is* Wednesday, then the others might come while I am gone, and I will have to explain why *I* am now late. Plus, I might have to answer a lot of questions over at the library. It has completely slipped my mind that if it *is* Tuesday, the library (which is closed on Tuesdays) will not even be open. A closed library would prove it is Tuesday, but I do not think of that. I could go outside and ask a passerby what day it is. But that would just confirm any latent suspicion that might be floating around town regarding my state of mind.

I am feeling a little foolish now. If today is Tuesday and not Wednesday, what will I say to someone from church who might spot me as I leave and ask me what I am doing at church on a Tuesday night? I am getting uneasy as I think about my daughter finding out about my predicament. Would she become concerned about me being out without supervision? No, she would not. She would laugh. Very hard.

I am finally forced to admit to myself that I have no idea what day it is. I have narrowed it down to Tuesday or Wednesday, but it is a ten-mile drive back home, so I really need to get this pinned down rather soon. I cannot go wandering the streets asking people what day it is. Should I pack up and head for the car? What if it *is* Wednesday and somebody comes while I am driving away? I really need to know right now what day it is.

I look around. Pulpit, piano, pews, bulletin board, hymn books, oil stove. Aha. The timer on the oil stove will have the date on it, but will it tell me what day it is? I squint over the top of my bifocals and bend to read the digital display and, what do you know, right next to the date and time in the lower left corner of the tiny, wonderful screen, there it is: "Tu". I straighten up, push my glasses back, zip up my Bible cover, and try to decide if I will share my funny little story with the folks at church tomorrow night. That is, if tomorrow really is Wednesday.

UPDATE: Wednesday morning, June 14, 2017—I can't find my purse.

UPDATE: Wednesday night—Found the purse. I left it at the church on Tuesday.

48 GOD MEANT IT UNTO GOOD

*And we know that all things work together for good
to them that love God, to them who are the called
according to his purpose. Rom. 8:28*

God's word teaches that it is a father's duty to bring up his children in the nurture and admonition of the Lord. A loving father will observe his child carefully and, by God's grace, relentlessly weed out anything in the child's heart that should not be there. He is not obligated to explain all his actions to the child. The child's duty is to trust and obey his father, knowing from experience that his daddy has his best interest in mind. Sometimes the process is painful. But the father does what is necessary because he loves his child.

Likewise, the business of growing in the Lord, of maturing and becoming more Christlike, is sometimes a painful and messy ordeal. Our heavenly Father may gently teach us all our life, but the time comes for all His children, when a specialized tool, a more exacting method of loving discipline, is needed. The right tool must be used for the job or the desired result will not be attained.

Our Heavenly Father loves us and desires us to be in close fellowship with Him. He wants us to become more like His son, Jesus, and He knows exactly what is required to accomplish His purpose. If we refrain from fighting Him during the process, trials and affliction will bring us closer to God and help mold us into His image. Here is an illustration:

My husband, Manfred, is in the business of restoring log homes. Sometimes, the work that is necessary for repairing a house can appear, well, catastrophic. But, in order to properly repair and preserve the house, he must get down to clean, sound wood. He must search out and destroy all the weak, rotted, crumbling wood wherever he finds it. He must do whatever is necessary to save the house. He cannot simply cover up the deterioration with new stain and hope for the best.

Sometimes the process is brutal and, inevitably, the job site will become strewn with piles of rotted wood, sawdust, plastic sheeting, tools, loud machines, buckets, scaffolding and hoses. Manfred might even make temporary gaping holes in the walls.

Occasionally, a homeowner will get anxious at the sight of so much apparently senseless destruction. From their perspective, it appears Manfred is demolishing their home. They wonder if they have made a terrible mistake or if the roof might fall in. The work seems to take an awfully long time and they wonder if this project might cost more than they are willing to pay. The damage seems irreparable.

But then they recall checking the references of this person who is creating a royal mess in their life and they find his record to be reliable. They have visited other houses where Manfred has worked his restoration wonders and have found the finished projects to be sound. They begin to relax and trust the expert and the entire process becomes much less stressful for them. Some begin to delight in the adventure and start snapping pictures.

And so it is in life. Faced with what appears to be catastrophic destruction, trusting the Expert can be difficult. The key is to have confidence that our heavenly Father knows what He is doing. We must read His Word and check His record and continually remind ourselves of His reliability and of His goodness.

Then, resting in Him, we can know with firm assurance that, *to them that love God, to them who are the called according to his purpose*, *all things work together for good*.

~~~

How wide is this assertion of the Apostle Paul! He does not say, We know that some things, or most things, or joyous things, but ALL things—from the minutest to the most momentous; from the humblest event in daily providence to the great crisis hours in grace. And all things work—they are working; not all things have worked or shall work; but it is a present operation.

<div align="right">MACDUFF</div>

Divine Providence is a downy pillow for an aching head and a blessed salve for the sharpest pain. He who can feel that his times are in the hand of God, need not tremble at anything that is in the hand of man!

<div align="right">CHARLES SPURGEON</div>

49 TRUST GOD? WHY SHOULD I?

You are suspended from a rope over a yawning chasm. Your climbing partner has just plunged into the abyss right before your eyes and has met with a terrifying, horrible death. And there you are, alone and afraid, twisting in the wind at the end of your rope, stunned at the demise of your friend.

What happened? Did my friend's rope fail? Will mine? Will I end up smashed to pieces on the rocks, too? Was I sold an inferior, defective length of rope? How stupid we were to trust a skinny bundle of fibers with our lives! Fear and doubt creep into your mind and, because you no longer trust it, you cut the rope that holds you, the only thing connecting you to safety.

In the wake of child loss, it seems many parents, even believing parents, find their trust in God severely shaken. They may become angry at God or hold themselves at a distance from Him. They are reserved in their relationship with Him or may stop praying or attending church. They open the Bible and stare at the words without reading. Some conclude God has betrayed them.

This is not how it should be. The hard work of grieving and sorrowing should be a time when trust is solidified, like a concrete footing curing on a foundation of bedrock. Bereavement can and should be a time of spiritual growth. But true growth is not something we can experience without God's help. If we fight Him, life becomes much more difficult than it needs to be as we compound our sorrow with doubt and anger, creating problems in our relationship with God and with others.

Sure, you can get back to the business of living, pull yourself up by your bootstraps and "move on", as they say. You can "survive". But, unless we trust the Lord and have confidence that He does all things well, we can never become more Christ-like. Without trusting Him and the plan He has for us and our children, we will not be receptive to the full measure of the grace He is waiting to pour into us.

Trusting God is not a "just do it" kind of thing. It is a gift God bestows on a well-prepared soul, one that has been carefully cultivated by the Spirit of God and taught the attributes of God from Scripture *before* the loss occurs. When you know and believe who God is and what He says about Himself, you have a rock-solid foundation on which to stand when the great sea billows of life crash over you. Knowing Him well is the best and only preparation for whatever life throws at us. God's truth, His *trustworthiness*, is the pillow upon which we can rest our head in the still hours of the night. Anchored to Him, His truth permeates our sorrow, infusing it with the blessed aroma of His peace.

But what about those who have been blind-sided by loss, completely unprepared? Those who are now groping in the dark for something, anything, to muzzle the catastrophic pain. They crawl among the shards and splinters of their heart looking for answers, gazing at photographs, glassy eyed in astonishment, wondering...

How could this have happened? To Me?

And in their pain, they wall up their heart, denying access to the only One who can help them. They cut the rope.

I know of parents who firmly believe their children are in Heaven and plan on joining them there someday, but at the same time, they are furious at God and want nothing to do with Him. Trust God? *No, I do not. When I get to Heaven, I will find my child and go spend eternity somewhere in the no-God-allowed section.*

So, what is the answer for the unprepared? The answer is still God. He can meet you in an instant right there in your pain and show you the wonders of Himself. There is no one else you can trust completely because people are just people. Only God is God.

The alternative to trusting God is to not trust Him, not believe Him. To deny His power, His love, His existence. Not trusting Him means I must trust something else, some other person or god or man-made "ism." But there *is* nothing else. There is nothing and no one that delivers what God can deliver: Blessed assurance. Sure hope. Peace that passes all understanding.

Trust in myself? I am a person of average ability. If I wanted to and I worked hard enough, I could probably be an executive, or a journalist, or a teacher. I can bake nourishing bread. I can organize the un-organizable. I am a decent shot with a firearm. There are many things I can do—important things. But I cannot raise the dead. I cannot bring our son back.

If I cannot trust God, or if He does not exist, then I will never see Hans again and there is no purpose for anything that happens, either good or bad. In fact, with no God there *is* no good or bad other than what I decide for myself and what you decide for yourself and what evil people decide for themselves.

By definition, God is good, and God is love. Therefore, everything He does is good. I trust Him on that basis. I do not trust that He will do what I want or spare me pain. I do not trust what I believe *about* Him. I trust *Him* because He is wise, and He loves me.

I do not trust in my limited understanding, but in God, the One who knows best. Our son is safe and happy with the Father. Our separation is temporary. I will see him again. God's Word says so. God cannot lie, so I can trust what He says.

I am hurting and will always hurt to some degree. I do not want to waste any of this pain. I want to extract all God has for me in this colossal thing that has happened to us, missing none of the lessons. *This must not be for nothing.*

With a full and hurting heart, I want to be the one singing the loudest, smiling the brightest, loving the fullest so that God gets all the glory. This will take time, I know. But I want it known right now that **our Lord is worth it**. Knowing Him is everything and trusting Him is easy because He is Holy and True and Faithful and Good.

How can I *not* trust Him?

50 GOD'S PROMISE: PSALM 49:15

> *But God will redeem my soul from the power of the grave: for he shall receive me. Selah. Psalm 49:15*

It was Christmas Eve, just a few weeks before he turned four, that Hans received Jesus as his Savior and Redeemer. This means Hans counted on nothing other than the shed blood of Jesus, who died in Hans's place, as payment to a Holy God for his sin. Jesus' sacrifice of Himself and victory over death (when He rose from the dead) is Hans's guarantee of entrance into Heaven. Sin, death and the grave have no power over Hans and when Jesus returns, all we who know Him will receive new, indestructible (redeemed) bodies. Then we will all be together again. And so shall we ever be with the Lord.

> *But I would not have you to be ignorant, brethren, concerning them which are asleep, that ye sorrow not, even as others which have no hope. For if we believe that Jesus died and rose again, even so them also which sleep in Jesus will God bring with him. For this we say unto you by the word of the Lord, that we which are alive and remain unto the coming of the Lord shall not prevent them which are asleep. For the Lord himself shall descend from heaven with a shout, with the voice of the*

archangel, and with the trump of God: and the dead in Christ shall rise first: Then we which are alive and remain shall be caught up together with them in the clouds, to meet the Lord in the air: and so shall we ever be with the Lord. Wherefore comfort one another with these words. 1 Thess 4:13-18

The Roman Road to Salvation in Jesus Christ

But God commendeth his love toward us, in that, while we were yet sinners, Christ died for us. Romans 5:8

For the wages of sin is death; but the gift of God is eternal life through Jesus Christ our Lord. Romans 6:23

That if thou shalt confess with thy mouth the Lord Jesus, and shalt believe in thine heart that God hath raised him from the dead, thou shalt be saved. For with the heart man believeth unto righteousness; and with the mouth confession is made unto salvation. Romans 10:9-10

For whosoever shall call upon the name of the Lord shall be saved. Romans 10:13

For God so loved the world, that he gave his only begotten Son, that whosoever believeth in him should not perish, but have everlasting life. For God sent not his Son into the world to condemn the world; but that the world through him might be saved. He that believeth on him is not condemned: but he that believeth not is condemned already, because he hath not believed in the name of the only begotten Son of God. John 3:16-18

51 SURVIVAL IS THE STARTING POINT

Initially, the pain of child loss is so severe it is easy to wonder if it is survivable. Many women say they know, if it happened to them, they could *not* survive it. But I want to tell them: *Yes, you can. If I can, you can. We have no choice. There is no option.*

However, here is something to think about: Yes, surviving is a good thing. But *just* surviving is not the ideal and does not mean we are growing. Surviving is not enough. Just because I have survived does not mean I have grown.

Yes, I am still standing. Now what? *What does God want me to do with this?*

> *Now our Lord Jesus Christ himself, and God, even our Father, which hath loved us, and hath given us everlasting consolation and good hope through grace, Comfort your hearts, and stablish you in every good word and work. 2 Thessalonians 2:16-17*

God has so ordered, that in pressing on in duty we shall find the truest, richest comfort for ourselves. Sitting down to brood over our sorrows, the darkness deepens about us and creeps into our heart, and our strength changes to weakness. But, if we turn away from the gloom, and take up the tasks and duties to which God calls us, the light will come again, and we shall grow stronger.

J.R. Miller (1840-1912)

The dark brown mould's upturned
By the sharp-pointed plough;
And I've a lesson learned.

My life is but a field,
Stretched out beneath God's sky,
Some harvest rich to yield.

Where grows the golden grain?
Where faith? Where sympathy?
In a furrow cut by pain.

Maltbie D. Babcock

52 WHY THE GRIEVING SHOULD GO TO CHURCH

And let us consider one another to provoke unto love and to good works: Not forsaking the assembling of ourselves together, as the manner of some is; but exhorting one another: and so much the more, as ye see the day approaching.
Hebrews 10:24-25

Since Hans left us, attending church has sometimes been difficult for me, even though over twenty months have passed since the crash. But, right from the start, I purposed in my heart that I would not let the enemy of my soul enjoy one iota of satisfaction by getting me to stay at home when God's people meet.

Yes, it is hard, a real emotional workout sometimes. But the longer I sit there fighting the tears (or sometimes just letting them fall) the more victorious I am. If my heart is right, the adversary gets zero victory as I stay right there in the pew, no matter how much I may want to flee.

Sometimes I sit there out of pure obstinance: *No Satan, I will not run, I will not let you smirk at one of God's hurting children while you whisper, "Where is your God?" This is my pew. I am not budging.* There is strength and safety in numbers; by God's grace, I will persevere among the Lord's people.

Hans died on a Monday evening. Our family was there at church two nights later for Wednesday prayer meeting. We were there the following Sunday for morning worship. Our daughter was the church pianist at the time and played for us that morning as usual. I know I could not have done it. But, on that first Sunday morning without our Hans, amazing me as she often does, she played for us, dry-eyed; and I was so proud of her. As for me, it took all I had just to get through the singing. Sometimes it still does. Self-control while falling apart, is a hard discipline to master.

The words to the hymns now have deeper meaning for me. Hymns about grief and pain and sorrow are extremely challenging, and I struggle to sing them. I try to keep my tears under control because once they start, it is hard to stop. I am, however, greatly encouraged by the livelier hymns that proclaim the blessed hope of our returning Savior. Our bright and glorious eternity with Him is what I prefer to sing about.

> Oh, the dear ones in glory,
> how they beckon me to come,
> And our parting at the river I recall;
> To the sweet vales of Eden
> they will sing my welcome home,
> But I long to meet my Savior first of all.
>
> FANNY CROSBY

I do not always cry because of sadness or because I miss Hans. Often I cry because when we are singing the great hymns of the faith, particularly the songs about Heaven, I am overwhelmed by the magnitude of what God has accomplished by sending His Son to die for us and by the blessings He has in store for us in our eternal home. When the saints are singing around the world on a Sunday morning, the glory of Heaven seems a whisper away. *And Hans is there!*

Hallelujah is more than a word on the page to me now. I can barely utter it without weeping. It is my heart cry, my connection with Jehovah's holy throne and with the saints gathered round about it (including our Hans!).

When we sing the old hymns, the entire family of God throughout the ages are together, unified in our praises and unshackled by the constraints of time. I can almost hear them singing with me from every corner of the planet and I feel an upward pull in my spirit toward my Father's house. It is a taste of the joy to come. I feel I am late for the party.

Ours is a small church and in this little frame building our family has accumulated over twenty-five years of memories—precious memories but sometimes distracting. I raise my head from the hymnbook, and they come flooding in:

Hans, who was not even remotely musically gifted, was our song leader for a time (he referred to himself as The Number Caller-Outer) and I still look up at the pulpit and imagine him standing there in his gray suit, calling out the numbers and (successfully, I assured him) trying not to look nervous. During the sermon, he would sit right in front of us, where now there is an empty pew.

In another pew, I see scratch marks in the wood, made by his suspenders when he was a little boy. His crayon box from Sunday school, with his named misspelled, is still on the shelf with the others.

I look up at the ceiling and know there is insulation above it which he blew in there a few years before he left us for Heaven. I imagine him straddling the rafters with the hose. Beneath my feet, under the floor, are sheets of insulation which keep the cold from creeping up into the building, and I think of him battling spiders in the crawlspace so his claustrophobic dad wouldn't have to.

In the fellowship room, the foosball table is quiet. Out the window is the parking lot where I last spoke to him face to face. Yes, sometimes it is hard to go to church.

But it is home. The prayers of our brothers and sisters in the Lord strengthen us and we are built up through the preaching and teaching of the Word. We are thankful the Lord gives us grace to love each other despite our flaws and misunderstandings. Together we worship our Heavenly Father in times of rejoicing and in times of trial. God has given us the high privilege of fellowship, with Himself and with His people. The grieving need to be in church.

Yes, it might be messy. It will probably be painful. And I know how easy it would be to stay home. Forsaking the assembly saves some of what precious little energy you have. It saves you the embarrassment of crying in front of people. It saves you from awkward social situations, from questions, from insensitive comments, from the pain of your child not being there, from no one saying his name, from being misunderstood.

But staying home robs you and others of some things. It robs you of an opportunity to affirm that our strength comes from the Lord, and to be a testimony of His care for us. It robs the skeptic of the chance to observe how a Christian handles a painful trial. Your very presence demonstrates that God is good and worth the hard work of being in public when your heart is demolished. Your praises make it evident to the powers of darkness that we worship God because of Who He is, not because of what He gives us or from what He spares us. I believe a hurting, sorrowing Christian who has resolved to sit in the pew and worship no matter what, can be a beacon of hope to others who are, or who soon will be, in a season of trial.

God's church has always had sufferers in her midst. There is no shame in this. In fact, suffering can be a ministry; those who have suffered tremendous losses before me, have ministered to me in ways they will not know until we meet in Heaven. I believe some of them have *the gift of suffering*. Their walk with the Lord during affliction shows me that, in the Lord, I can do this. How could I see and learn this if the suffering saints stayed home to spare themselves the hardship of appearing in public?

There is little benefit to withdrawing from fellowship when we are hurting. But there is great value in doggedly going to church regardless of the severity of our pain. Unbelievers, new believers, and the angels themselves need to see us worship God during the tough times, not as a testimony of our "strength", but as a testimony of God's goodness, worth and majesty.

So, I want to encourage the sorrowing, the grieving, the hurting believer, to do the hard thing. *Go to church.* Get some of your heavier crying done on Friday or Saturday. Then, on Sunday, plunk down a fresh box of Kleenex™ next to you on the pew and claim your spot in the congregation of the redeemed. It is good for you, and it is good for The Church.

Do not let the enemy cheat you out of this blessing. Ask the Lord for grace and strength to obey and honor Him by worshipping in the assembly of His people—even when it hurts. Especially when it hurts.

Worship that means something, costs something. Be a good soldier. Do the hard thing and go to church. For Him.

> *Praise ye the LORD. I will praise the LORD with my whole heart, in the assembly of the upright, and in the congregation. Psalm 111:1*

~~~

Believers are free from condemnation but not free from pain, sickness, poverty, losses, crosses, sudden trying changes, and what we call premature death. These trials give occasion for the exercise and manifestation of many graces which are not so visible in the sunshine of prosperity. Our trials are further sanctified, to wean the people of God more from the world, and to weaken the body of sin which still dwells in them.

<div align="right">JOHN NEWTON</div>

53 WHY RELIGION DOESN'T HELP

Religion means different things to different people. I do not consider myself to be a religious person. I am a Christian. A Believer. A Bible Believer. I might even be a Baptist. I go to church every week to worship and hear the Word of God preached. But I would not refer to myself as religious. The word is too imprecise and, in our culture, loaded with connotations.

When structured as a human-centered system, "Religion" or even "Faith", cannot provide substantial relief for the pain of bereavement because the focus is misplaced. There is no anchor, no solid comfort, no immutable absolute by which you can measure your experience. Religion (false religion) cannot provide an accurate way for you to get your bearings in the midst of the storm. The rules are different depending on what culture you are in and change with the passage of time.

Undoubtedly, religious practice makes some people feel better. But I need more than that. For me, the *facts* of my faith (Who God is, what He has accomplished and promised) and my *relationship* with Him give meaning and life to my grief. I still hurt—a lot; but it is not a destructive, senseless, purposeless hurt. Jesus loving me and carrying me—this is what I depend on over time as I move through this experience with Him. I worship the God who is real, the One who knows me and saved me from sin and death. I worship the all-powerful One who can and will bring Hans back someday.

I firmly believe there is a purpose and explanation for every tragedy; we are not always privy to what they are. But God knows, and that is good enough. I do not believe in accidents and I do not demand explanations; God either causes or allows everything for His purposes; we are simply not capable of seeing the big picture as He sees it. Too often, evil seems to win. *We* would do things differently and we expect God to treat us better because we have been so devoted, so religious. But that is not how it works. God does not owe us anything.

We must remember, it is not about *us* or our religion. It is about God. And not only does God know what He is doing with the universe He created, God wins in the end. Life and Love have already triumphed over death and sin, or where is our hope?

Unfortunately, there are alternatives to having a living relationship with the living God. There is hopeless, godless, creation-worship. Or devotion to a reckless, whimsical, powerless, counterfeit, nebulous, non-personal "higher power" that cannot help us. We can shop around and choose some combination of these to create our own personal, my-way designer religion.

But I could not hang on to that thin a thread for very long. Mere religion does not do it for me. If you have tried religion and it has done nothing for you, I want you to know there is a better Way.

There is Jesus

54 BETRAYED

Betrayal is the act of violating the trust or confidence of another. It is to be false, faithless, treacherous. To betray is to abandon, desert, deceive; to lead astray; to deliver to an enemy by treachery; to fail or desert, especially in time of need; to be unfaithful in guarding; to disappoint the hopes or expectations.

Often the bereaved feel God is guilty of these things because they expect things of Him He never promised. They feel His plan should line up with their plan. They feel that because they love, follow and serve Him, they should have gotten a better deal and they become angry when He does not deliver according to their expectations.

We had hopes and expectations for Hans. We are disappointed we will not get to see Hans live out his life here among us. But we are not disappointed in God. The Lord's plan for Hans is not the plan we imagined. But because God is God, we have full confidence that His plan is the best plan. God's plan is good and perfect because God is good and perfect. We hurt because we miss Hans. But at no time have we added to our pain by doubting God's goodness or wisdom. For this mercy, we are inexpressibly thankful.

It is no secret there is an abundance of suffering in the world. I live with the pain of child loss and, as too many know, it is no small trial. But when I read the news or hear horrendous stories of what is going on in other countries and even right here in the lives of my own coun-

and neighbors, I am brought face to face with the fact that multitudes of people have it way worse than I have.

I do not know all the whys and hows of God's plan in this suffering world. But I do know God, and *that is the key*. I know I can rely on His goodness, love and wisdom to make this all come out right. He has promised no one a pain-free life. He *has* promised never to leave us or forsake us.

> *for he hath said, I will never leave thee,*
> *nor forsake thee. Hebrews 13:5*

Suffering one, God has not abandoned you. He will not fail you. He operates even now to bring all things to their final consummation. God is working His plan, and it is good. It is going to be alright.

May I make a suggestion that may help you? Get your Bible and start reading. Ask Him to show Himself to you. He claims to be trustworthy; ask Him to show you that. If you are questioning His wisdom, ask Him to show you His wisdom. If you wonder if He truly is good, ask Him to show you His goodness.

And pray. Confess to Him your anger and disappointment in Him. Receive His forgiveness for doubting Him. Acknowledge to Him that He is God, and you are not. Ask Him to give you the trust and faith in Him you need to be at peace with Him. This is one prayer, if asked with proper motive and attitude, He delights to say *yes* to.

> *I will not leave you comfortless: I will come to you.*
> *Peace I leave with you, my peace I give unto you:*
> *not as the world giveth, give I unto you. Let not*
> *your heart be troubled, neither let it be afraid.*
> *John 14:18,2*

Grieving mother, sorrowing father, God heard you begging for your child's life. Yes, He could have healed your baby. In love and wisdom, the answer He gave was *no*. If God is good, and He is, then this was the best answer He could have given.

Oh, how this hurts our heart! But in the storm of this terrible pain, there is Jesus. He is there hurting with you, sorrowing because His child is in deep, doubting heaviness. Go to Him when the pain is so bad you do not think you can take another breath. Go to Him and find rest for your battered heart. He can bring relief in an instant. And then, when the pain crashes over you again, return to the One who can help you bear it. Again and again go to Him. There is no other Comforter. None.

If we know God, if we are taught accurately from the Scriptures and believe what He says about Himself, angry feelings melt away and trust takes its rightful place. I miss my boy, too. The pain is still there. This is not about becoming pain free. This is about knowing God and receiving the peace only He can give.

~~~

> Ah, God! behold my grief and care. Fain would I serve Thee with a glad and cheerful countenance, but I cannot do it. However much I fight and struggle against my sadness, I am too weak for this sore conflict. Help me in my weakness, O Thou mighty God! and give me Thy Holy Spirit to refresh and comfort me in my sorrow. Amid all my fears and griefs I yet know that I am Thine in life and death, and that nothing can really part me from Thee; neither things present, nor things to come, neither trial, nor fear, nor pain. And therefore, O Lord, I will still trust in Thy grace. Thou wilt not send me away unheard. Sooner or later Thou wilt lift this burden from my heart and put a new song in my lips; and I will praise Thy goodness, and thank and serve Thee here and for evermore—Amen.
>
> S. Scheretz (1584–1639)

55 JOB'S WIFE

> *Then said his wife unto him, Dost thou still retain thine integrity? curse God, and die. But he said unto her, Thou speakest as one of the foolish women speaketh. What? shall we receive good at the hand of God, and shall we not receive evil? In all this did not Job sin with his lips. Job 2:9-10*

Job's wife is a mystery lady. Scripture gives us the name of Job's daughters, but not the name of his wife. There is no background information about her and no real follow up either. We know she was chosen to be the bride of a very upright and successful man. God blessed her with prosperity and a home filled with children. It is probable that she was respected and admired in her community. I am sure she received the same care and attention from her husband that he gave to their children. Until her infamous *"curse God, and die"* moment, there is no evidence that she was any worse a helpmeet than the rest of us.

So, what happened? What led her to allow her tongue to be used to tear down her husband, just when he needed her most?

"Dost thou still retain thine integrity?" Why do you continue to serve God? Where has your righteousness gotten you? Look what He has allowed. Look at our life. Everything is gone. Our children are dead. Your flesh is putrid. We have followed God all our lives, and this is what we

get? Fearing God and leading an upright life has gotten done.

And then she says it. She urges Job to do the very predicted Job would do if God took away all he had: *"touci hath, and he will curse thee to thy face."*

"Curse God and die," she says.

And then Job responds to her with the exact, God-breathed words she needed to hear at that moment: *"What? shall we receive good at the hand of God, and shall we not receive evil?"* Do we serve Him only because He blesses us with peace, safety, and goodness? Shall we not accept whatever He is pleased to allow in our life? Does disaster change who God is?

God gave Satan permission to touch all Job had; He placed all but Job's life into Satan's power (Job 1:11-12). That would include Job's wife. What better way to really get at Job and provoke him to curse God than to incite his own wife to forsake him in his desolation? However, despite his wife's defection, *"In all this Job sinned not, nor charged God foolishly." Job 1:22*

So, how does a person come to a place where they succumb to the pain of loss and fall into a bitter rage against the Almighty? I doubt if Mrs. Job was in the habit of cursing God. Perhaps this was a brief and terrible moment of doubt, fear, and bitterness that welled up and spilled over onto her husband as he sat there in the ashes. Maybe in her overwhelming grief she lashed out in a way that was entirely out of character for her. After all, boils presumably excepted, Job's wife suffered the same trials as Job.

Or perhaps she felt betrayed. Perhaps she felt she and Job deserved a better deal. Maybe she enjoyed the benefits of being the wife of patient, prosperous Job without herself ever having much of a relationship with the God of her righteous husband.

Was she a habitual self-absorbed shrew, or was this just a moment of weakness? It is hard to tell from Scripture. I find it interesting that Job offered sacrifice on his sons' behalf (and presumably his daughters') but not for his wife (Job 1:5). Was he confident that she herself kept close accounts with God? We just do not know.

So back to my original question: What happened with Job's wife? What led her to allow her tongue to be used to tear down her husband, just when he needed her most?

It seems this woman had her eyes focused on the devastation around her and could not, or would not, see God's hand in it. Possibly, she was comfortably accustomed to blessing and prosperity and was shaken to discover that bad things happen to "good" people, too. She had not yet learned, as her husband soon would, that God has the right to do what He wills *because He is God*. If only she had run to the truth that the sovereign Creator is thoroughly trustworthy and that everything He allows in our lives works for our ultimate good.

When your world flies apart and none of it makes sense; when pain overwhelms you and you begin to doubt God's motives and to speculate on the truthfulness of His Word and the integrity of His character; when Satan whispers God does not care about you, that He is not the good God you thought you knew, that this devastation is all there is for you—remind yourself of the facts: *God is good, and He loves me. He is wise and in control.* That is all you need to know.

Whether God causes our loss directly, or allows Satan a free hand to inflict pain and suffering, should we not count it an honor to be chosen to honor *Him* in our adversity, to prove to a hurting world that our God is worthy to be praised in all circumstances? If we can be thankful for nothing else, can we thank Him for allowing us the honor of praising Him in our pain?

Both believers and unbelievers need to see real flesh and blood people of God following hard after Him during the rough times. Not because He is a Santa Claus or a crutch for the unthinking. No, they need to see we follow God because He is *Wonderful*. By God's grace, this is what we as believers are called to do.

Job's faithfulness forever settled the question at the heart of Satan's accusation:

> *Doth Job fear God for nought? Hast not thou made an hedge about him, and about his house, and about all that he hath on every side? thou hast blessed the work of his hands, and his substance is*

> *increased in the land. But put forth thine hand now, and touch all that he hath, and he will curse thee to thy face. Job 1:9-11*

With the prompting of the Adversary, it is easy to focus on our suffering instead of remembering *who this God is* that we have been praising all the days of our abundance. Job (and hopefully his wife) recognized this and found peace:

> *I have heard of thee by the hearing of the ear: but now mine eye seeth thee. Wherefore I abhor myself, and repent in dust and ashes. Job 42:5-6*

God is good when things are going my way, and He is good when things are not optimal. God is good when life is smooth and peaceful, and He is good when calamity strikes. That God allows painful things to happen does not change who He is. We can waste an awful lot of time and energy trying to figure out why God allows suffering, questioning His motives, and doubting His goodness. Let us not speak as the foolish women speak. Let us praise Him for who He is, not just for what he gives us. And if, in His love and wisdom, He takes away all that is precious to us, let us *worship* and say with Job:

> *the LORD gave, and the LORD hath taken away; blessed be the name of the LORD. Job 1:21*

Do not wait to feel it before you will say it. Say it because it is true.

> *Wherefore also we pray always for you, that our God would count you worthy of this calling, and fulfil all the good pleasure of his goodness, and the work of faith with power: That the name of our Lord Jesus Christ may be glorified in you, and ye in him, according to the grace of our God and the Lord Jesus Christ. 2 Thessalonians 1:11-12*

56 THAT WOMAN

You may have met her. That woman. The one who has an incurable health problem and has only months to live. Whose husband has run off and shamed her. The one with the wayward teen. The one whose child died.

You may have met her, that woman who is living your worst nightmare. I remember seeing her around several times. Before. But, back then, I did not understand her. At all.

For one thing, she is smiling. A lot more than I would if I were her. And she never complains. She hardly ever brings it up, this nightmare of hers. She keeps up with all her usual duties and on top of that, she often does more than her share. She should be a wreck, but instead she goes out of her way to comfort others. She says things like, *God is good*, and seems so nauseatingly thankful all the time. What is wrong with her?

She must still be in shock. Or denial. Maybe she is taking a little something to help get her through this. Maybe what she has been through isn't so bad or she doesn't have enough sense to understand what has happened to her. Maybe she's just strong. Maybe she drinks.

Or maybe it's something else. I hear she's religious. Maybe there's something to that Bible-thumping stuff and that Jesus-talk isn't just a crutch for non-thinkers or an anesthetic for weaklings. Maybe she's got something real there to hold on to. Perhaps I need to check this out. What's up with this woman?

No, skeptical one, it is not shock, nor denial. What this woman has been through is bad, unbelievably bad, and she feels it in every bone of her body. But she will not give up. She will not hand the final word to the enemy of her soul, so he can snicker while another Jesus freak bites the dust.

What you see in this woman results from time spent with God. You are seeing Christ in her. She is operating under the power of the Holy Ghost. Her ship is powered by Someone Else's fuel. I am sure this woman takes her sorrow to her Lord regularly and then wipes her eyes, blows her nose, and gets back to the business of blessing others. She refuses to waste the pain. She is bearing fruit. And I want to be like her.

Those of us who have lost a child know that those who have not suffered a similar loss cannot understand what we are going through. So, while I continually feel a need to spill my guts and try to make people understand the magnitude of my pain, I don't do it. I don't do it because there is nothing they can do for me and they and I both know it. Death is a problem of Biblical proportions. Only the Creator of the universe can handle this one. So, when people ask me how I am doing, I say *I am fine*, or *I'm OK*, or *I'm alright* (or sometimes, *I'm pretty good*), because to tell it like it is would be, for the hearer, like I am speaking a foreign language.

And sometimes I simply say *God is good* and I say it for several reasons: First, it is true. Second, I want people to *know* it is true. And third, *knowing* He is good makes it possible for me to smile and go around saying *I am fine*.

I'm fine is no lie. I admit I am in pain, a drop to your knees and scream kind of pain. But I am fine because I know, without a doubt, that God is infinitely Good and that I will see my sweet boy again.

That woman. Maybe I am beginning to understand her.

57 WHAT IF?

> *O LORD, I know that the way of man is not in himself: it is not in man that walketh to direct his steps. Jeremiah 10:23*

In the aftermath of devastating loss, it is natural to speculate, to retrace the preceding events, to root around in the morass known as, *What if?*

What if I had called or texted her an hour earlier?
What if I had not left him alone?
What if the doctor had not been negligent?
What if I had gotten him to the hospital sooner?
What if I had paid closer attention to all the warning signs?
What if she had turned right instead of left?
What if, just before the crash, I went over to look at the work Hans did on his car and said hello, instead of hurrying to the house to wrap his birthday presents? *What if* [insert one of a million possibilities]? *Would things have turned out differently? Would my child still be alive?* These are unanswerable questions. We must yield to not having the answers and rest in the promise that we will understand it all when we see the Lord.

What if? is a particularly wearing question because we cannot understand or see all that God is doing on the larger scale. There are too many variables, repercussions, and influences that we have no knowledge of—*yet*.

The way I see this is, if it happened, and God knew beforehand it would happen, and He did not intervene to stop it from happening, then He allowed it, or, perhaps in some cases, even directly caused it. Nothing takes God by surprise. There are no *What If?*s with God.

Being preoccupied with *What If?* does not help us and cannot change the outcome. What happened to your child may not be good, but God *is* good and, since He operates from an eternal perspective and with perfect wisdom, we can depend on Him to always do or allow what is best. He has all variables and possibilities under His control.

The grief and pain I suffer does not make God happy. But, since He knows the end of all things, as well as what is best for all of us in every circumstance, I can trust that the departure of our son was not a random, meaningless event. It was precious in the sight of the Lord. I can be confident that 1/11/16, shortly after 6 p.m., was the appointed time for Hans, because God knows every hair on my boy's head. God alone decides life and death. A sparrow cannot fall to the ground without His knowledge. I do not need to ask, *What if?*

What If? concerns the period of time before the loss. Some of us can look back to the days, hours, or minutes preceding the departure of our children, and clearly see what is now so very evident, but went unnoticed or unheeded at the time. It may have taken the form of a smile, a look, a comment, or a sort of something-is-going-to-happen feeling that rose up in our gut. It may have been more of an impression, not necessarily unpleasant; an apprehension, an awareness of the need to pay attention or to say or do something. But we dismissed it because it was so vague; we have had feelings like that before and nothing terrible happened.

In the days and weeks, even years, before Hans left us, I had a feeling like that more than once—the last time just minutes before the crash. As my husband and I rolled into our driveway that evening, upon our return home from an overnight trip, I felt a pull to walk over to Hans and say hello as he was finishing up working on his car. This one small act on my part would have delayed his leaving for the highway by enough time for the pickup that hit him to pass by the crash site. So, did I miss a *What If?* opportunity, a chance to change the outcome?

No. I still believe Hans would have died at that same precise moment. Perhaps an aneurysm, or unexplained seizure, or rolling his snow machine, or maybe his car or a tree falling on him would have been the instrument. No, it was Hans's appointed time and no *What If?* action on my part could have changed that.

As I hurriedly scooped his presents off the back seat of the truck so he would not see them, my gut was telling me something was happening that I could not stop. Everything appeared to be normal, but I felt like I was closing a door or turning a corner, the corner that separates *then* from *now*. The moment felt... pivotal. But my rational mind was telling me *Hans will come to the house in a few minutes and you can say hello and give him his presents then. Just go to the house.*

So I did. Looking back, it all seems so *arranged*, as if we were being moved along according to schedule. To me, that anticipatory impression seems now to be a sort of trans-time phenomenon, as if the future sorrow about to engulf me was spilling over into the present moments leading up to the crash, as if the sequential order of events was temporarily blurred and everything was happening *now* or had already happened.

What If I had walked over to Hans and engaged him in a two-minute conversation, delaying his departure and thus "causing" him to miss meeting and colliding with the other vehicle? This is foolishness. I do not have that kind of influence. My *What If?*s have no substance and no power. They are fabrications.

I believe the Lord steered me away from Hans and over to the house that night to spare me additional pain. The shock of seeing him alive and vigorous one minute, watching him drive away, and then hearing the crash and knowing, knowing... *that* might have been too much for me. My decision to go to the house did not cause the crash. Hans's decision to test drive the car did not cause the crash. I do not believe our actions that night determined God's appointed time.

Could it be the *What If?* questions we ask *after* a traumatic event and the anticipatory moments we experience *before* the event are related? In retrospect, I can see it all coming and I get the feeling time is not as rigid as we imagine it to be. It is amazing to me now to see how God's plan unfolded with such care and precision.

So, why does *What If?* haunt us? We torment ourselves with *What If?* because we feel we should have acted on those anticipatory impressions, vague as they were. We think we could have done something to thwart death and hate our inability to control it. We think we can protect our children from it—that there is *something* we could have or should have done. We punish ourselves for not knowing the future and cannot accept that, faced with death, we are powerless.

There is no full and satisfying answer to *What if?* and when we stumble down that road, we are seeking something that does not exist. The answer to *What If?* is elusive because it is infinite. Every shift in circumstances causes a chain reaction of new variables. Even if God gave us the knowledge we seek, we could not comprehend it. And we would still miss our children. They would still be gone.

Give the *What If?*s over to God. They are too heavy for you to carry. In eternity, He will make His purposes known. He loves you and He has got it all worked out.

~~~

Jesus knows how His followers can best serve Him. He sent the apostles out to teach and heal. John the Baptist, however, He permitted to be seized, to languish in prison, and to be cruelly beheaded. Just so, we should be willing to serve our Master in any way He desires. He may want us to give a long life to active usefulness—or He may want us to serve and honor Him by enduring persecution and being murdered. The life of John seemed to be a failure. He preached only a few months! He was a great preacher, too, and hundreds went to hear him. It seemed to his friends a pitiful waste of life, an irreparable loss to the heavenly kingdom, when he was murdered. But John's work was done. He accomplished all that he was sent into the world to do. There really was no reason for his living an hour longer. When one dies in youth, we are apt to deplore his death as untimely. But God makes no mistakes! "Every man is immortal—until his work is done!"

<div align="right">J.R. Miller (1840–1912)</div>

58 WHY?

Another common question after loss is: *Why?* Yes, there is sin, death, and suffering in the world, and so it will be until Jesus returns. But *Why me?* many want to know. *Why my child?*

There is no simple answer to *Why?* The life and death of an eternal being cannot be neatly packaged, labeled and placed on a shelf. The *Why?* questions cannot be resolved by analyzing all the possibilities and reducing them to straightforward conclusions. And even if they could be, would that make everything all better? *Why?* is God's business. It is a God-sized question. A better question is, W*hy not me?*

Every life touches so many others, not just in proximity but over time. Just as a new life (no matter how brief) changes everything, so too, when that life departs, the loss impacts not only the character of the immediate family circle but, well, the course of history. Only when we meet our Lord face-to-face will we finally know the influence our child's life and death had on the world. Every person's life, no matter how "short," *matters*. It changes the dynamics of the sphere into which it was born.

Likewise, a child who departs before birth or shortly after, leaves a profound impression on the people who love it, on extended family and friends, on caregivers, and on those who are merely observers. A child not born is a loss to all humanity. God uses the lives of departed children, including those in obscure and seemingly insignificant circumstances, in ways known only to Him.

God may choose to bless some parents with evidence of His working through the lives of their departed children. It may be someone will get saved or encouraged because of the testimony a child left behind. Perhaps an unbeliever might consider his own mortality and eternal destiny when confronted with the stark reality of death. But I think most of us will not see a fraction of God's intricate and wonderful plan surrounding the lives of our children this side of Heaven.

If God were to provide us with a full explanation of *Why?* we simply do not have the capacity to comprehend the complexity and enormity of it. Knowing this helps me because it verifies what I already know: losing a child is huge.

I think this is why we may become irritated when a well-meaning person attempts to furnish reasons for why our child died. They want to help, and they feel compelled to come up with something, anything, that will offer hope and comfort. They may actually need to answer this question more for themselves than for you. If they can discover the answer to *Why?* then maybe they can avoid having what happened to you happen to them. But we (and probably they) instinctively know there is no simple answer to a question as colossal as *Why did my child die?* It hurts even to suggest an answer. We may have moments when no reason seems good enough.

Thankfully, I have not been plagued with wanting to know *why* God called Hans home so unexpectedly. I have spent much time trying to understand *how* it happened, but I do not have the energy to tackle *Why?* I leave the *Why?* question with God. I trust He knows what he is doing, and I know He always does what is best. My pain does not change that.

59 FORGETTING

Can a woman forget her sucking child, that she should not have compassion on the son of her womb? yea, they may forget, yet will I not forget thee. Behold, I have graven thee upon the palms of my hands; Isaiah 49:15-16

There are things about Hans I will never forget for as long as the Lord grants me a sound mind. The day of his birth, the day of his death, and the many precious days in between. But like scripture memorization or math facts, if we do not rehearse and review what we have embedded in our mind, it fades and is forgotten. Or is it?

The brain is amazing. I have heard of elderly people whose dementia has ravaged their minds to the point of not recognizing loved ones, yet if you sing them a song they learned seventy years ago, they will sing it right along with you. The memories, though tangled and hard to access, are still in there.

When our son with Down syndrome suffered a regression in cognitive function, we were concerned that he might have forgotten everything we had worked so hard to teach him. But, after he recovered, we were relieved to discover he had retained almost everything. It took work, but in time, things learned years ago were brought back up where he could use them when he needed them. It was all still in there.

That the memories of the details of life with my boy are fading, is a reality that hurts. At first, I was panicky about forgetting things. Grasping in desperation, I tried to hold on to all the memories at once. In my mind, I scrambled to stuff all that was Hans's life into a virtual Rubbermaid™ container so I could be sure of access day or night, always and forever. (My *actual* Rubbermaid™ container is under our bed). I began a list in a spiral notebook of things I feared I might forget. I crawled through photo albums, inspecting the backgrounds of old family photographs, mining for memories.

Eventually, I stopped my daily examinations of the photo albums because I found I was beginning to carry memories of photographs instead of genuine memories of actual events; the pictures were actually making me forget. So now I prefer to look out and around and remember things that happened in certain spots around our home or in town. I use the photos as a supplement to memory and not as a substitute.

But it is not just the smaller details of *Hans's* life that I am forgetting. I am forgetting many details of *all* our lives. That's just normal. We cannot avoid forgetting the minutiae of daily life that makes up the cumulative body of our families' histories. Each day, each hour we have together, is packed with the small moments that make up life: a man-sized fistful of flowers, a boy-sized Lincoln Log™ fort, the milky smile of a nursing babe.

It is the commonplace memories I treasure most, and they are the ones that are often forgotten first—mostly because there are so many of them. It is customary to snap pictures at major events, but some of my favorite photos were taken on ordinary days when we were doing ordinary life. I treasure pictures that were taken when no one was paying attention to the camera. Those grainy candid shots capture evidence in the background of the goings-on for that day.

It is not possible for me to remember everything about every day that Hans was with us. I forgot many of the memories years before he left. Perhaps I should have been more meticulous about recording everything. It would be nice to have a larger stash of tangible memories.

Much as we would like to, we cannot remember everything. Before photography, videos, answering machines, tape recordings, cell phones, cloud storage, and scrap-booking, one might have only a lock of hair or a small portrait of their departed. One picture on the wall or in a locket—that's it. That and what the years recorded in the heart. Maybe it was easier that way. Maybe we are supposed to forget?

But even if I do "forget" some things (can a mother *truly* forget?) God does not. I believe He has all the memories stored up for me and will bring them to my recall as needed for the rest of my life. I fully expect Him to sprinkle my thoughts with precious memories, one by one, as gifts to me as we walk this road without our Hans. Memories of smiles and laughter; of crashing Legos™ on the wood floor; of the quiet roll of his voice in the evening and the slow sparkle of his eyes.

Every now and again, the Lord brings something to my memory that I had not thought about in years. He gifts me with a "forgotten" memory of our son and it is such a delight, not only because I get to remember, but because I know God gave the memory. That means the precious details of our life that I thought were long forgotten, and the ones I worry might *be* forgotten, are safe with Him, and I do not need to fear they will be lost.

It is over two years now since I have laid eyes on Hans. But if I turn from memory to hope, I see I am more than two years closer to seeing him again. It is a discipline to think about it this way, but I must keep this fact in front of me: The separation is temporary.

The physical body Hans occupied was a confinement, a snapshot, if you will, of all he truly is. Much as a photograph is just an image, the material physical presence of our son, along with his will, emotion, intellect, and personality as we experienced him, was just a temporary place for him to be. The real, perfected version, with all his potential fulfilled, is currently and actually safe and present with the Lord. And I *will* see him again—in just a little while. I am on my way to him. I am just not there yet.

Hans is not a fading memory; each day brings me closer to him. The photo is not fading, it is being developed. New memories are in our future. And *that* lovely reality outshines every photograph I now weep over.

60 BUT GOD GOT HIS SON BACK

Some feel that because Jesus rose from the dead, God the Father did not experience the grief one associates with child loss or that the death of His Son, Jesus, was easier for Him because of His foreknowledge of the Resurrection.

It is astounding to think that God the Father and God the Son were willing to endure the death and separation of the cross while Jesus was made sin for us. *Made sin—for us!* In the darkness, while Jesus cried, "My God, my God, why hast thou forsaken me?" the anguish of the moment exceeds anything I can comprehend. It was an unprecedented break in a holy fellowship that had known no interruption for all eternity. This, so I could be reconciled to my Father God.

> *For he hath made him to be sin for us, who knew no sin; that we might be made the righteousness of God in him. 2 Corinthians 5:21*

Was God's pain less than mine? I think of my worst moments of painful grieving and realize that what the Godhead experienced during the crucifixion and death of Jesus was *infinitely* worse. Yes, three days later (our time) Jesus rose from the dead. But, for Father God, the shame of sin placed on His Son, and the grief of death's darkness, were infinite orders of magnitude worse as experienced by an infinite, holy God. For this was the horror of eternal separation compressed into the forsaken hours of sin-bearing agony on the cross. If sorrow was quantifiable matter, the pressure would be incalculable. And only an infinite God could shoulder the infinite weight of it.

Yes, God knew His Son would be resurrected; God got His son back. I know my son will be resurrected; I will see him again. This knowledge is a tremendous comfort to me, but it does not eliminate the pain of our current separation. And I do not think it negates the pain the Father knew as His Son suffered and died while bearing my sin and yours on the tree.

For the child of God, death is a victorious, joyous homecoming. But it is also a departure. For those of us still earthbound, saying goodbye always brings tears. God sees and feels our sorrow. He is no stranger to grief. God the Father has seen the death of countless of His children throughout the ages and the sorrow of those who grieve them. God has experienced child loss countless thousands of times.

The death of God's Son, Jesus, did not come cheap. I do not believe my pain is greater than His simply because His Son was gone "just for the weekend."

That's just how I see it.

~~~

In one thousand trials it is not five hundred of them that work for the believer's good, but nine hundred and ninety-nine of them, and one beside.

GEORGE MUELLER

What we have once enjoyed deeply we can never lose. All that we love deeply becomes a part of us.

HELEN KELLER

61 SUFFERING: A PERSPECTIVE

Remember them that are in bonds, as bound with them; and them which suffer adversity, as being yourselves also in the body. Hebrews 13:3

One of the neat things about blogging on the internet is that people from around the world can read what I write. For someone such as myself, who remembers the invention of hand-held calculators, this is slightly mind-blowing.

Astonishing as this is to me, it is also sobering. I write primarily with my own culture and worldview in mind. But I know my blog has readers from a great variety of backgrounds, circumstances, and nationalities—from China, Nigeria, Kenya, Zimbabwe, Ukraine, Nepal, Saudi Arabia, Israel, Kazakhstan, Pakistan, Uganda, Turkey, Iraq, and many other far-away places.

With that in mind, I want to clarify my use of the word *suffering*. Those who have lost loved ones through sickness, accident, suicide, or other terrible circumstances experience intense grief, pain, and sorrow. We *suffer*.

But to those who live in tough places, I want to acknowledge that I understand the difference between suffering and *Suffering*. As a nation, we Americans rarely experience the suffering seen in many other parts of the world. Yes, we suffer here—a brief glance at the news or at what goes on inside a neighbor's home daily, will confirm that. We have had our wars, shootings, acts of terror, and natural disasters with all the terrible suffering that accompanies those events. But, when we Americans, myself included, use this word *suffering*, I cannot help but wonder what people beyond our borders think of us, the people who live with intense *Suffering* every day.

I do not want to minimize anyone's pain. Child loss hurts. A lot. I am offering a perspective, not making comparisons. But I believe we sometimes use this word *suffering* too carelessly. I have referred to my experience of losing a child as "suffering", and so it is. But I suffer, if I can call it that, in a snug little cabin in one of the most beautiful places on the planet. I hurt, but I do it with a full stomach, in peace and safety with friends, loved ones, and medical care nearby.

When I look out into the sea of humanity, I feel uncomfortably self-focused using this word *suffering* so freely. Yes, I suffer, but in my mind, *Suffering* looks more like this:

> KIDNAPPED NIGERIAN GIRL WILL NEVER BECOME A MUSLIM, FATHER SAYS (WWW.WORLDWATCHMONITOR.ORG)
>
> "They gave her the option of converting in order to be released but she said she will never become a Muslim," Sharibu said. "I am very sad but I am also jubilating, too, because my daughter did not denounce Christ."

Or this...

> AN ESTIMATED 120,000 UIGHURS ARE BEING HELD IN CHINESE POLITICAL REEDUCATION CAMPS IN KASHGAR PREFECTURE ALONE
>
> "The camps, usually located in converted government buildings and schools, are overcrowded. Officials routinely send detainees to different locations (including prisons) without telling their family members, RFA reported. In one camp, cells that once held eight people now hold fourteen, and detainees need to sleep on their sides in order to fit. Some have reportedly been seen walking in the camps without shoes despite below-freezing temperatures."

Or this...

Held 5,128 Days—Twen Theodros Arrested March 2004 in Eritrea (www.prisoneralert.com)

"Twen is an amazing Christian woman who endured terrible beatings and torture at the hands of Eritrean prison guards. On occasions, Twen took the punishment in place of Helen and, when Helen was very ill as a result of the beatings and prison conditions, Twen cared for her. She fed Helen, washed her wounds, defended her and even carried her to the toilet when Helen was unable to walk."

Or this:

62 STRENGTHENED ACCORDING TO HIS WORD

*My soul melteth for heaviness: strengthen thou me
according unto thy word. Psalm 119:28*

Doctrine: that which is taught; scriptural teaching on theological truths.

One of the potential positives of bereavement is the opportunity it provides for a healthy examination of one's beliefs and long held, but untried, assumptions. For me, child loss has been galvanizing. Every doctrinal truth I had been taught about my Father God, the entire foundation of my faith in Christ Jesus, was solidified the instant I heard the words *Hans is dead.* The lightning bolt that cleaved my heart, in the same strike, fused the Truth of God's Word and the reality of His love to the very core of my being.

I know this is not how it is for everyone. The Lord ministers grace to each of us in exactly the way needed. There is no one-size-fits-all way to do child loss, and I claim no special privilege. I am not sure how I would have held up under a lengthy period of doubt and so I am thankful the Lord made it crystal clear to me that Hans's homegoing was undeniably from His hand. That dreadful night, God gave me a gracious gift of instantaneous (though far from painless) assurance, straight from His heart to mine.

I believe the Lord enabled me to receive this gift so readily because He had, through the ministry of the Holy Spirit, and "the foolishness of preaching," carefully prepared my heart in the years leading up to Hans's departure. Year in and year out, verse by verse, line upon line, the Spirit of God graciously used the faithful preaching and teaching of His word to lay an unshakable foundation that has allowed me to keep my footing even as the earth seemed to move beneath me.

So, why is sound doctrine important for the bereaved (and for the not-yet-bereaved)? Because doctrine is important to God. "Rightly dividing the word of truth" promotes right thinking and growth. When a believer has the Word of God and the indwelling Holy Spirit as Teacher, Comforter, and Friend, bereavement can be a profitable time of shedding the erroneous and appropriating the True. Child loss, like any trial, can raise a lot of questions in the hurting heart. The answers rarely come easily.

Questioning one's beliefs about God is beneficial when asked with a searching and humble heart. Questions are a normal reaction to catastrophe. But fist-shaking rebellion and blaspheming unbelief is sin and helps no one, especially not the griever.

No matter what you feel, His Word is still true.

UNKNOWN

Sorrow can refine us and help us grow stronger. But compounding one's sorrow with inaccurate notions regarding God's sovereignty, goodness and love gives our Adversary a formidable weapon. He can and will use the resulting feelings of anger, betrayal, doubt, and abandonment to shred our faith to little pieces. A distance can develop between our broken heart and our Lord, Who desires to heal us and bind up our wounds.

For some, bereavement can be a season of disorienting disequilibrium and it may take some time to wade through the confusion to a place of growth, acceptance, and peace. Time in the Word, time in prayer, and time alone with God is what it takes to get there. If this sounds like work, that is because it is. It is part of the hard work of grieving.

Grief is not an illness or a weakness; it is not that we work to get rid of it (as if that were possible). Being sad because your child died could not be more normal, and it is crucial to understand that pain does not equal spiritual failure. Sorrow, within the framework of right thinking and a right relationship with God, is a tool in His hand for our good.

When we think right, our emotions will eventually follow. There have been many occasions when I have been able to deflect an emotional meltdown by stopping my thoughts in their tracks, redirecting them to God's promises, and then running His Truth through my mind until the grief-wave passes. This does not eradicate the pain, but it does help keep it under control for those times when a good cry is not logistically possible. When I keep my emotions in perspective, in the light of the promises found in God's Word, I can hear His voice, feel His presence, and know He is at work. I can grow rather than wither.

Wrong thinking about God and about how He operates is a serious handicap to growth and healing and can add years to our recovery. Making feelings a priority in our post-loss life, rather than making the Lord and His Truth our priority, is a serious mistake. Feelings cannot be trusted and following your broken heart has the potential of leading you to a very bad place.

Focusing excessively on the pain of the loss, rather than thinking right thoughts about God, creates more pain. We risk becoming disappointed in anyone who does not sufficiently acknowledge or accommodate our emotional fragility. Relationships suffer. We become victims instead of victors.

While sound doctrine lays the foundation for right thinking, and right thinking facilitates growth and healing, it is also important to remember that right thinking without obedience, and obedience without love, are nothing more or less than hypocrisy. Without a right relationship with God, the whole thing comes crashing down and there are bound to be casualties.

Sound doctrine protects the griever from error and deception and from spiraling into despair. Knowing God, pursuing an accurate knowledge of His Word, and believing what He has said, clarifies our perspective and gives us the eyes of gratitude that see His loving hand in all things. For the hurting heart, this is the way of peace.

> *Thou wilt keep him in perfect peace, whose mind is*
> *stayed on thee: because he trusteth in thee.*
> *Isaiah 26:3*

The grieving are vulnerable. Sometimes we cannot think straight. We forget to pay bills. We find it hard to engage in small talk. Some become so desperate to numb the pain or to recover what they have lost, they find it hard to resist temptations they would ordinarily flee from, such as drugs or alcohol or consulting a psychic medium. Satan knows this, and he has no scruples about exploiting the weak, the hurting, and the helpless.

It pains me to see loss parents grieving harder than they ought because they do not know the Word. They have adopted erroneous ideas about God or have been heavily influenced by the constant barrage of contemporary cultural misinformation. The ubiquitous, anti-God, anti-Christ, *it's all about you* media bombardment of our day is no help. It has led us to believe that happiness is the goal and prosperity is the measuring stick of spiritual success. Friends post happy, pain-free selfies; we continue scrolling, feeding the idea that if we are suffering, we necessarily must be doing something wrong.

Some believe we deserve and are promised a pain-free life because we are Christ-followers. God has promised no such thing. God's people can and do suffer—they always have, and they will until Jesus returns.

> *That no man should be moved by these afflictions:*
> *for yourselves know that we are appointed*
> *thereunto. 1 Thessalonians 3:3*

The more lies the griever believes, the more she will suffer. The more she understands God's character, Who He is, and what He says, the lighter the burden will be. To be ready for a hit like child loss, we must forsake the wishy-washy *God is my pal and He wants me to be happy* theology so prevalent today. If we can worship God in the middle of life's devastations, we bring Him honor. We proclaim His worth. We declare the fact that we worship Him because of who He *is*, not because following Him makes life rosy.

God is Love. He is my Friend; He knows my frame and that I am dust. He keeps track of all my tears and understands my sorrow. He knows I am weak and tired and so very sad. But that does not give me license to wallow in it. It is wrong to presume upon His compassion so that I make excuses for my sour face or ugly temper.

> *It is good for me that I have been afflicted; that I might learn thy statutes. Psalm 119:71*

It is not wrong to have feelings of deep sorrow and crushing grief, especially in the early months and years. It is healthy and necessary to experience the whole scope and depth of the loss. But it is counterproductive to coddle emotions such as self-pity and hopelessness, which only bring us down further and extend our pain to others. I cannot make it all about me. To do so puts me in spiritual danger.

I am not the first to suffer a loss; I will not be the last. I will not abandon myself to despair nor whine as if God's plan is a poor deal. I do not need pity, for I am *blessed*, chosen to bear a light affliction for His name's sake, and I look forward to a far more exceeding and eternal weight of glory. This is His promise, His unfailing Word.

> Christianity is a way of life founded on doctrine. Some disparage doctrine in favor of the spiritual life. Paul, however, taught that spiritual growth in Christ is dependent on faithfulness to sound doctrine, for its truth provides the means of growth (Col 2:6). The apostle John developed three tests for discerning authentic spirituality: believing right doctrine (1 Jo 2:18-27), obedience to right doctrine (2:28-3:10), and giving expression to right doctrine with love (2:7-11). Faithful obedience and love, then, are not alternatives to sound doctrine. They are the fruit of right doctrine as it works itself out in the believer's character and relationships.
>
> Baker's Evangelical Dictionary of Biblical Theology. Edited by Walter A. Elwell Copyright © 1996 by Walter A. Elwell. Published by Baker Books. (Used with permission under "Fair Use")

God is holy and just. He is wise, and He is true. The Lord is gracious, and full of compassion; slow to anger and rich in mercy. He never changes, and He loves His children with a love we cannot fathom. He keeps His promises. *I can trust Him.* These facts, taken together, are my starting point.

I start by believing God is holy and good and He loves me. Knowing this to be true, I can see clearly all He allows in my life (or in my loved ones' life) has purpose and works together for good. I am then in a position of trust and can proceed from there to praising Him and giving thanks to Him in everything. From there, everything else falls into place. This is not what people expect from the bereaved, and they take note. God is honored.

> *My lips shall utter praise, when thou hast taught me thy statutes. Psalm 119:171*

If I start with myself and my pain instead of with God, I get stuck in the Slough of Despond. My pain may obscure the facts I know about God. The Adversary can now gain a foothold in my heart. I begin thinking wrong thoughts about my Heavenly Father, and it shows. Others notice. God is dishonored.

What is the remedy? *A firm hold upon accurate teaching from God's Word, the Bible, and faith in the One Who wrote it.* To be optimally prepared for the devastations of life, we must *know* Him, and we must *believe* what He has said. We do not need to be theologians to reap the blessings of sound doctrine, but what we know needs to be correct. A firm grounding in the basic truths surrounding the person and work of God the Father, God the Son (Jesus Christ) and God the Holy Spirit is what we need to weather the storms of life. A correct view of God is fertile ground where the seeds of faith can grow.

> *... he who believes what he knows, shall soon know more clearly what he believes.*
>
> C.H. S<small>PURGEON</small>

I can face today's trial because I stand on a foundation of Truth, firmly anchored to the blood-washed, unshakeable bedrock of the gospel of Jesus Christ. Without God's Word and sound teaching from it, without the facts regarding His character, without the promises, without the Holy Spirit of God, I would be a puddle of faithless despair. But, because I know and believe Him, I can say without any doubt that the true and living God is real, He is good, and He is worthy to be praised. By His grace, may I never give occasion to the Enemy to bring dishonor upon my Lord and His holy name.

It is good to be able to answer gainsayers; but we cannot do so if we know not the Lord Jesus clearly and with understanding.
C. H. SPURGEON

So, what do I need to know? I need to know God is good and He loves me. *I can trust Him.* Repeating it does not water down the Truth that everything God does or allows is motivated by His love for us.

Who can tell his height of glory then? And who, on the other hand, can tell how low he descended? To be a man was something, to be a man of sorrows was far more; to bleed, and die, and suffer, these were much for him who was the Son of God; but to suffer such unparalleled agony—to endure a death of shame and desertion by his Father, this is a depth of condescending love which the most inspired mind must utterly fail to fathom. Herein is love! and truly it is love that "passeth knowledge." O let this love fill our hearts with adoring gratitude and lead us to practical manifestations of its power.
C.H. SPURGEON

I need to know that God is God, and I am not. Life is often unfair. I am not the center of the universe, and neither is my pain. It is not about me. God's plan is all about Him and His Glory. We chafe at this because we are self-focused. As we walk around inside our own skin, we view everything that happens to us through the lens of self: *How does this make me feel? How does this impact my life? Why did this happen to me?*

So then, is God self-focused when He asks us to honor and glorify Him? He would be if He were not holy and just. But because He is perfect and sinless, we can trust that what He requires is not only reasonable but is the best possible course. He has our best interest in mind at all times. Of whom else could this be honestly said?

I must view every event in my life through the lens of "Thus saith the Lord." It is God's universe, and He makes the rules. I do not have to understand them or even like them, but not believing them is foolish and irrational. If God is *God*, He *must* know what He is doing. It is best to just relax and let Him run things.

Understanding that God is good, and that He is the sovereign ruler of the universe, are two great truths for the Christian to think upon when preparing for or coping with the storms of life. But there is so much more to knowing God. We need to seek and support teachers of the Word that understand and value sound doctrine. Ask the Lord to lead you away from false or compromising teachers and to bring godly encouragers into your life. Look for a group of believers who can help you understand the hard sayings of Scripture and help you steer clear of error. And pray. The Lord honors a sincere heart-desire for His truth. He wants you to know Him.

How sweet is rest after fatigue! How sweet will heaven be when our journey is ended.

GEORGE WHITEFIELD

63 AS TIME GOES BY

Contrary to various cultural notions, there is no set timeframe for grieving. None of us "gets over it" in the one year (or less) of mourning that is often allotted to us. Each family, and every member in it, operates within a unique set of circumstances that will influence both the weight and duration of heavy mourning.

Early in my grief, the sorrow, longing, and anguish felt like a connection to Hans. To remember him was to *be* with him. Now, though the Lord has carried me through two-and-a-half years of missing my boy, I still sorrow. It is just as heavy as ever, but I have grown used to carrying it. Grief is no longer great waves crashing relentlessly over my head; it is more like quiet little waves that lap continually at my heart. It is not as sharp and overwhelming as it was in the early months, but it is still there, a part of me.

Grieving, in the early months of bereavement, is hard, healthy, exhausting work and is a necessary part of our healing. There is no getting around it; it is work we must do and no one can do it for us. However, it is important to remember that grieving excessively can become counterproductive if indulged in too deeply for too long. Life does in fact go on whether we want it to or not. Our Father wants us to be a part of it. He wants us to live, not just exist.

But it is not easy. Loss of a loved one affects every facet of our lives: relationships, sleep patterns, physiology, emotions, energy levels, spiritual issues, mental health, appetite, memory, family dynamics, finances, and so much more. It is a tsunami that leaves a diverse and disorienting array of wreckage on the sunny beach that was our former life.

Is it any wonder then, is anyone still truly surprised, that we cry so often and so easily in the first months and years of child loss? Tears are often the only way to release the astonishment one feels in the face of disaster. In the beginning, tears come almost continually, sometimes with frightening ferocity. You sense you could get lost in this storm and not even care.

This hard grieving of the newly bereaved is agonizing but, as in childbirth, the pain can be productive. As bad as it was, I felt it moving me to some new and better place. I was not enjoying the experience, but the labor felt constructive—it felt *right*. It hurt terribly, even physically, but it was something I needed to do. Later, I learned to plan episodes of grieving in advance: *I will wash these dishes and then go cry for five minutes before starting dinner.*

Those early grief-storms, the intense crying, the wailing, all help to process what has happened to us. We are tossed and battered until, exhausted, we are thrown into the arms of our Heavenly Father where we can rest awhile until the next wave hits. Fragments of pain are purged from our heart and the shrapnel is flung overboard. Tears of release float us to a quiet place where we can function again. We sleep, eat, produce a few smiles, and resume daily operations for a while before the storm returns. And then we do it again. And again. This is the life of the parent who has lost a child.

But incredibly, time passes. You notice the waves roll onto the beach at less frequent intervals than before. You feel a little less conspicuous, a little less fragile. The churning rawness begins to abate, not because the pain is less, but because you become too worn out to cry. Slowly, you realize your tears will not bring your child back, and this knowledge brings fresh sorrow. But your sorrow gets quieter, burrows deeper, becomes part of you rather than something you do battle with. Your sails are in shreds, but you are afloat, becalmed and drifting to who knows where.

More time passes, and you smile at the memories, rather than fall apart. Instead of seeing empty places where your child should be, you see God's hand as you look up with awe, knowing your believing child is *up there*. And you accept the truth that Heaven is the best place for him to be.

~~~

God does not desire us to waste our life in tears. We are to put our grief into new energy of service. Sorrow should make us more reverent, more earnest, more useful. God's work should never be allowed to suffer while we stop to weep. The fires must still be kept burning on the altar, and the worship must go on. Grief should always make us better and give us new skill and power; it should make our hearts softer, our spirits kindlier, our touch more gentle; it should teach us its holy lessons, and we should learn them, and then go on, with sorrow's sacred ordination upon us, to new love and better service.

<div align="right">J.R. Miller (1840-1912)</div>

64 GRIEF: KEEPING OUR EMOTIONS IN CHECK

A sapphire and golden September day; a cup of tea with my husband; a visit from our daughter; Sunday worship or evenings with our remaining boys still at home—all these give me a warm and cheerful peace. The sadness is still there under the surface, but it does not dominate every moment.

Then there are those other times. Times when it is hard to be with people; hard to listen to their problems or smile at their successes. Hard to get the social momentum going. Hard to care.

When you are hurting, it takes a lot of energy to stay involved in the lives of others in a meaningful way. But with God's help, we can do it. He commands us to love one another, to love our neighbor as our selves. This loving of others can take many forms, but mostly it involves putting others first and doing what is best for them, sometimes at your own expense.

It might mean having a good cry two days before a social engagement so you can show up dry-eyed on the big day and not spoil the pictures. Sometimes it means withholding a smart remark while listening patiently to someone mourn the loss of a cat. Sometimes it means bucking up and doing a job that needs doing even though your heart is hemorrhaging.

So, when I manage to arrange my face into a smile, or I muster up the energy to appear "happy," I am not denying my pain or wearing a mask. I am not disregarding or being disloyal to our son's memory. I am not trying to fake having it all together in the eyes of God or man. I am not sugar-coating child loss. To attempt such a charade would be ludicrous. What I am attempting to do is to put the giant named Despair out of the room and my own feelings on the back burner while trying to focus on the needs of the moment.

If I am truly counting my blessings and cultivating a thankful heart attitude, responding to *How are you?* with *I'm fine,* is no lie. I have lost much, but I still have way more than I deserve. *I'm fine* is actually an understatement and does not begin to cover the myriad blessings God has bestowed on our family. *I'm fine* seems meager compared to God's great and merciful dealings with me. I am astounded that He is pleased to accept my paltry *Thank You, Lord.*

Smiling and maintaining my "OK" for the sake of another's comfort (or my own), is not being a cold-hearted stoic or being fake. It is exercising the grace of self-control for the honor and glory of God. It is an offering, a testimony to the power of God's sustaining love and the veracity of His Word. It is being other centered instead of self-centered. It is modeling the fact that God is sufficient to comfort me to the point of composure, quiet acceptance, contentment, peace and joy.

This does not mean we can simply choose to be cheerful. To be honest, cheerful is not my default right now. No, we must come to God and ask Him to help us, to impart His peace, His joy which is a different thing altogether than happiness. Regular time spent with Him in His Word and with His people produces an out-flowing of the real thing—the joy of the Lord.

At first, joy may be only a sporadic trickle, a drop here and there. Or it may come, like grief, in overwhelming bursts. It may look different in different people. In some it may resemble a delightful, bubbling brook. In others, it manifests as a tranquil pond you barely notice. But, if the Lord gives it, it will be the genuine article.

Am I there, yet? No, I am not, and I am mainly writing these words for my benefit. The discipline of grieving is not a grace which is acquired instantly. It is difficult to be a student in the school in which it is taught. The lessons are hard and sometimes long, and we fear we may never graduate. Sometimes we feel like dropping out.

But the Holy Spirit of God, the Comforter, is a tender and patient Teacher.

To those around me, I offer the best I can do in God's strength. The wrenching pain I bring to Jesus in private. Yes, often my motive is to avoid the embarrassment of crying in front of people and so maybe I am proud. But I do not think I should be encouraged or even pressured into letting it all hang out in the name of being real (whatever that means). This is not heroics. It is self-control.

The bereaved should not be made to feel that if they are not displaying the requisite vulnerability so fashionable these days, they are not then properly grieving, or that they are not processing their grief in a healthy way. I am not obligated to prove by my tears, to anyone, that death is horrible—I think people get that. Nor do I need to show them the dregs in the bottom of my cup to prove that God is able to lift me out of despair. And even if I were to share my pain whenever and wherever it hits, to whom would attention truly be drawn?

I cannot make the non-bereaved comprehend the pain of child loss sufficiently to satisfy my need for understanding, and so I should not get bent out of shape when they do not get it, or they quit trying. Sharing the full impact of my pain and telling them how the Lord has met me in it may be useful, but can never impart to them, in an effectual, internalized way, the lessons regarding the sufficiency of God's power to comfort and heal. I can witness to the fact that He does and allay their fears to an extent, but there is a limit to what others can learn through reading or hearing about other people's encounters with God's faithfulness. This lesson is something we must learn in the fires of first-hand experience. Reading or hearing about it is helpful and encouraging (or why write about it?). Seeing it lived out in someone's life is reassuring. Living it yourself welds it to your soul and makes it your own.

Spilling our emotional guts may not edify the non-bereaved the way we intend and trying to educate them usually proves unsatisfying. We expect from them more than they can deliver. They cannot feel what we feel and, unless the listener is extraordinarily wise and sensitive, unloading on them tends to confirm what they already suspect: *she's not handling this well at all; she's stuck; her mind is going; her faith is weak and worthless*, and so on. Even sharing deeply with another believer has a limit to its helpfulness—our experiences are all so different. I think that may be why child loss can be so terribly lonesome.

> *Though I speak, my grief is not asswaged: and*
> *though I forbear, what am I eased? Job 16:6*

The only way out of child loss is up. The best comfort we can give each other down here is to share the Word and to pray and weep together. The worst of our pain we must give to Jesus. Some roads must be walked alone.

So, I say little. I hurt no less when I keep my emotions in check, and any composure I exhibit should not discredit the reality and depth of my pain. But my responsibility is not to persuade others to accommodate the grievers in our midst with some imaginary safe space. Nor do I feel compelled to raise awareness about the supposed stigma surrounding child loss in what is termed "our broken western culture." Death, with its grief, is nothing new; every culture finds it shocking.

My responsibility is to praise God in the midst of my sorrow and to do it honestly and with adherence to His Truth. I hurt, but I reject victimhood. When I put on a happy face for you, I am not stuffing anything. I am not in denial or being dishonest or fake. Hopefully, instead of focusing on my emotions, I am focusing on God who grants me the grace to look beyond my own circumstances and gives me the strength to continue putting one foot in front of the other.

When you ask how I am doing and I answer *I'm fine* or *I'm doing alright*, I hope you will see right through me and my fragile smile, and into the heart and mercy of Jesus. I hope you will see His grace shining brightly just below the fractured surface of my soul and that you will give all the glory to Him.

65 THE STING OF DEATH

As one who is allergic to bee venom, I have a genuine appreciation for this word *sting*. The sting of a hornet (yellow jacket) has the potential to kill me and the only safe bee for me is a dead one, or one with no stinger.

> *So when this corruptible shall have put on incorruption, and this mortal shall have put on immortality, then shall be brought to pass the saying that is written, Death is swallowed up in victory. O death, where is thy sting? O grave, where is thy victory? The sting of death is sin; and the strength of sin is the law. But thanks be to God, which giveth us the victory through our Lord Jesus Christ. 1 Corinthians 15:54-57*

When Adam sinned, death entered the world and the sting of death, *sin*, began its deadly infection of God's very good creation. Sin has consequences, and every individual sin generates a new chain of more sin... *when lust hath conceived, it bringeth forth sin: and sin, when it is finished, bringeth forth death* and *the sting of death is sin* and on and on it goes, defiling, killing and destroying everything it touches.

Sin crucified the Lord Jesus. Sin—my sin and yours—is why our Savior died for us. As our Substitute, He took the death we deserve and gave us life in its place.

> *For when ye were the servants of sin, ye were free from righteousness. What fruit had ye then in those things whereof ye are now ashamed? for the end of those things is death. But now being made free from sin, and become servants to God, ye have your fruit unto holiness, and the end everlasting life. For the wages of sin is death; but the gift of God is eternal life through Jesus Christ our Lord.*
> Romans 6:20-23

> *Christ died for our sins according to the scriptures; And that he was buried, and that he rose again the third day according to the scriptures:*
> 1 Corinthians 15:3-4

Because of Christ's resurrection, the lethal sting of death has been removed, conquered, destroyed, rendered powerless. All my sin has been atoned for by Jesus, *who his own self bare our sins in his own body on the tree.* (1 Peter 2:24) So, for the believer, victory over death and over death's sting (sin) is an accomplished fact.

> *Verily, verily, I say unto you, He that heareth my word, and believeth on him that sent me, hath everlasting life, and shall not come into condemnation; but is passed from death unto life.*
> John 5:24

We live in a fallen world. People sin, and people die. Yes, death and sin are still buzzing around but they are in their death throes. Because I belong to Jesus, neither death nor sin has power over me. By God's grace, I can flee sin and pursue holiness. I still sin, but I am no longer the slave of sin. My flesh is still subject to physical death but, as a child of God, sin and death are but temporary problems, for God gives, has already given, the victory through our Lord Jesus Christ.

Sin gives death all its hurtful power. The sting of death is sin; but Christ, by dying, has taken out this sting; he has made atonement for sin, he has obtained remission of it. The strength of sin is the law. None can answer its demands, endure its curse, or do away his own transgressions. Hence terror and anguish. And hence death is terrible to the unbelieving and the impenitent. Death may seize a believer, but it cannot hold him in its power.

MATTHEW HENRY

When a believer dies, he attains the ultimate victory over sin and death. When temporal life claims its last moment, the believer leaves death, and its sting, behind and immediately enters into fulness of joy in the presence of the Lord. What was accomplished on the cross so long ago, is realized in all its splendor at the very moment we draw our last breath.

And because Hans belongs to Jesus, he claims this victory, too. He is today, right now, in a place where there is no sin, no sting, no death. His *body* rests in the grave, but death has no power over *him*. What may look like defeat—a brief life ending in a car crash—is, in reality, a *victory* in Jesus. What looked like defeat—a brief ministry in Galilee followed by a Roman crucifixion—was a *victory* over death *and* its sting.

The "saying" referred to in verse 54, *Death is swallowed up in victory*, comes to pass when we put on incorruption and immortality, exchanging our old vile body for our new glorious body. Though the ultimate fulfillment of this promise is yet future, it has already been secured for us in Christ at His resurrection. It is the fulfillment of Isaiah 25:8 and Hosea 13:14 which look forward to the Messiah, Jesus.

> *He will swallow up death in victory; and the Lord*
> *GOD will wipe away tears from off all faces;*
> *Isaiah 25:8*

He: Christ will by his death destroy the power of death, take away the sting of the first death, and prevent the second. In victory: so as to overcome it perfectly; which complete victory Christ hath already purchased for, and will in due time actually confer upon his people.

WESLEY'S NOTES FOR ISAIAH 25:8

I will ransom them from the power of the grave; I will redeem them from death: O death, I will be thy plagues; O grave, I will be thy destruction:
Hosea 13:14

Though in Christ, this victory is an accomplished fact, the full and final *consummation* of the victory over death will not occur until the Lord's return, when death will be destroyed forever. What a joyous, dazzling day it will be when we get our new forever-perfect bodies. Our old worn-out death-bodies will be transformed and death itself will be abolished, forever swallowed up in victory just as light swallows up darkness. And so shall we ever be with the Lord. Although they do not yet have their new glorified bodies, our departed, believing loved ones are enjoying the untainted blessings of incorruption and immortality *right now*. Is this not thrilling to think about?

The joyous outburst of the apostle, when he quotes the present passage (1 Corinthians 15:54), is the natural thanksgiving song of reassured humanity, on recognizing its final deliverance from the unspeakable terror of death and annihilation.

PULPIT COMMENTARY

But, meanwhile, back here on old planet Earth, until the day comes when we join those who have gone to Heaven ahead of us, we groan with grief, longing, disappointment, loneliness and sorrow. Our hearts are especially heavy if we have no assurance of our loved one's eternal state. These wounds are real, and there is no shame in bearing them.

But they are not the sting of death—*sin* is. Yes, sin brings forth death. However, that is not the end of the story. Death hurts for those who are left behind, and sin seems to rule the day but, for the believer, death in no way gains a victory. Its sting has been removed. Death, at its worst, serves only to usher us into the presence of God;

it can do no more. Where is the sting in *that*? The cross rendered sin and death defeated enemies—the empty tomb proves it. These Truths are real and there is no shame in declaring them.

> ... the Messiah shall by his death, and resurrection from the dead, obtain such an entire victory over death, not only for himself, but for all his people, that in the resurrection morn, when they will be all raised from the dead, death will be so swallowed up, that it will be no more...
>
> The prophet expresses it actively, it being a prediction of what was to be done by the Messiah; the apostle cites it passively, as being accomplished by him after the resurrection, and considered as a part of the song sung by the risen saints;
>
> But thanks be to God which giveth us the victory. Over sin the sting of death, over the law the strength of sin, and over death and the grave; and which will be the ground and foundation of the above triumphant song in the resurrection morn, as it is now at this present time of praise and thankfulness to God: and it is all through our Lord Jesus; he has got the victory over sin; he has put it away by the sacrifice of himself; he has finished and made an end of it; for though it reigns over his people before conversion, and dwells in them after it, yet in consequence of his atonement for it, it loses its governing power through the Spirit and grace of God in regeneration, and entirely its damning power over them, and in the resurrection morn will not be so much as in being in them; the view of which now fills them with joy, thanksgiving, and triumph.
>
> JOHN GILL

When reflecting on the phrase *sting of death* it is a powerful bolster to the hope of my heart to focus, not so much on the pain, the sting, or even on death, but on the *victory* over it and on the Victor.

When I sit at Hans's resting place, where this portion of Scripture was read on the day of his burial, I have an acute awareness that this piece of ground is not just his grave site but is his *resurrection site*. From this very spot of earth, Hans will someday come forth. He will have the same body—*glorified*. And not only that, *right now*, our Hans is incorruptible, sinless, victorious. Sin and death cannot touch him, much less sting him. *This* is the victory I rejoice and sing about.

At the burial service, though I was engulfed by the lacerating pain of loss, there was for me a clear moment of defiant victory when those words of triumph were proclaimed over Hans's vacant tent:

O death, where is thy sting?
O grave, where is thy victory?

These words acquire a new depth of meaning when you are staring down into the black hole that is your son's grave. When my husband, our remaining sons, and the other men reached for their shovels, these are the words that kept me standing.

On that day of staggering grief, as they lowered our Hans's body into the frozen ground, my heart was overwhelmed with the immensity of this new gulf fixed between me and my boy and by the overwhelming pull I felt (and still feel) to go to him.

But, based on trust in the shed blood of Christ and His atoning and substitutionary victory over death, *I sing*, knowing I *will* go to him someday because the sting of death has been annihilated. *That is the victory I possess in Jesus—right now.*

But thanks be to God, which giveth us the victory through our Lord Jesus Christ!

~~~

Death, to the believer, is but passing out of a world of sorrow and of sin—and entering upon a world of indescribable glory! If we lived more in anticipation of the happiness that waits us—earth would have less hold on our hearts' best affections.

MARY WINSLOW

66 HEALING AFTER CHILD LOSS

I still get those moments where I just cannot comprehend that Hans is gone from us. The difference now is the intensity. Those first weeks and months, and into the second year, the savage pain of those moments just immobilized me, saturated me. I did not know such pain existed. Back then, I fought to just keep my head above water and to simply breathe during the waves of crushing grief. Now, the main blast of the storm has passed over. The weather is still squally, but I am afloat and looking around for a place to beach my life raft. I still hurt from the beating I took in the water, and I am sad because Hans is not on the raft with me. But I know he is on the shore to which I am paddling. He is waiting for me. He is alive, safe, and happy; I will see him again. Thinking about that helps me to keep paddling.

I get tired sometimes and wish things were different, but that kind of thinking just makes things worse for me. I know now why in times past old women used to always carry a handkerchief. It was not just for decoration or to wipe children's noses, though it was good for that, too. No, rather, when you have lived long enough, it is likely someone dear to you has died. It was not uncommon for a woman to lose several children, sometimes all at once. When you are continually close to tears, when they are just under the surface of your smile, it is helpful to carry a handkerchief.

I still hurt, to be sure, and it would be very easy for me to spend much of my time looking at old photos and mourning what was. But too much time spent in grieving plunges me back down into the deeper parts of that ocean of pain. I do not want to be this sad for the rest of my life.

Child loss is so huge. The only thing bigger than pain like this is my Father God in Heaven. He has carried me through this. He is the wind in my tattered makeshift sail. And when His Son, Jesus, returns, *that* is the day I will see my Hans again (unless I die before then). Knowing this helps me to look forward.

Because looking backward all the time just hurts; I miss our old life. I miss our Hans. It hurts and it always will, but there must be more to life than hurting. I do not want to waste this pain by letting it destroy me or my relationships. I want to use it to help and encourage others if that is possible because there is a teeming world of hurting people out there.

When you are alone and you are weeping, and the longing for your child is a thick and expanding heaviness in your chest, threatening to erupt from your throat in silent, choking grief; when the missing him becomes a mountain of sorrow that looms over you as you whisper your child's name in astonishment, and it just *hurts*, hurts like nothing you have ever known before and you cannot escape it; when you feel trapped in the sadness and there seems to be no way out... Do not despair.

Sit and let it come. Be still and let it crash through your soul, toppling every idol as it surges through your heart. Let God do the work only He can do, purifying you, conforming you to the image of His Son. He is drilling, hammering, grinding, cutting away all that comes between you and Himself. *Of course* it hurts; do not run from it.

What does "healing" look like and how long does it take? I do not know. I do not even know if *healing* is the right word. Maybe the right word is *living*. Give yourself the time you need. Everyone's situation is unique, and "healing" looks different for each of us. I believe the closer we walk with the Lord, believing His Truth, the less painful this road becomes. I pray our Heavenly Father would grant you peace and healing as you follow His dear son Jesus into the lovely future found only in Him.

67 FOUR YEARS AFTER: SOME OF THE POSITIVES

*The LORD is my strength and my shield; my heart
trusted in him, and I am helped: therefore my heart
greatly rejoiceth; and with my song
will I praise him. Psalm 28:7*

Right from the first moments of our loss, I knew in my soul that my Father had a plan and a purpose for taking Hans to be with Him in Heaven. This did not lessen the astonishing pain but knowing that God is good and was in control of all things that day transformed Hans's home-going from senseless tragedy to glorious appointment.

While I cannot know with certainty what God's purposes are in all He allows in our lives, knowing He has a good reason for allowing it makes all the difference. I may not understand, but I can trust. I believe trusting God is key in reaping the blessings available to us when trials come our way. I am certain trusting Him is the way to peace.

I have written much about the pain of our loss—sometimes it's easy to get mired in the negatives. But I want to share here some positives I have experienced these past few years. Has it been *all* positives? Absolutely not. But it hasn't been all negatives either. Positives are possible. Here are some of them:

Since Hans left us for Heaven, I have gained...

- a stronger awareness of the reality of, and a longing for, my home in Heaven,
- a greater love for our Lord Jesus the Christ,
- a more constant awareness of His presence and love toward me,
- a more definite understanding that fear for my family's safety and well being has no power to affect the future,
- an acceptance of the fact that safety does not always look like what we expect,
- a realization that answers to prayer are far more intricate than we imagine,
- a sturdy appreciation of and a solidifying reliance on God's sovereignty,
- a quieter spirit,
- an increase in conviction regarding control of my tongue,
- a disgust for how often I "miss the way of love" (Amy Carmichael),
- a solid trust in God's providence,
- a firm knowledge that with God there is no danger and without Him there is no safety,
- a solid assurance that Hans is not "gone" or "lost." He is alive and he is Home. In the flesh, I will see him again,
- a fondness for the night sky,
- a surprising realization that sorrow is a joy and that grief can be beautiful,
- a deep sadness that keeps me from reaching hasty conclusions about people,
- a renewed appreciation and deeper love for my faithful husband and for our marriage,
- a profound gratitude for the children God has given us,
- a greater dependence on and confidence in the effectual outworkings of prayer,
- a hearty anticipation of the Lord's soon return,
- a calmer acceptance of His will,
- a sweeter appreciation for the beauty around me,
- a sober detachment from the shallow and trivial,
- a growing abhorrence for deceit and treachery,

- an awe for how God shows His love and care for me in very personal (and sometimes very spectacular) ways,
- a delight for birdsong,
- a deeper understanding of the great hymns of the faith,
- a stronger connection to and fellowship with the saints across the ages,
- a sense of peace and safety while reading God's Word,
- a sense of relief when my sin is exposed,
- a sense of wonder regarding the Lord's grace,
- a more defined recognition of my unworthiness,
- an unfathomable awe of the Lord's great love and mercy toward me.

> *... blessed be the name of the LORD.*

Safely Home

I am home in Heaven, dear ones;
All's so happy, all's so bright!
There's perfect joy and beauty
In this everlasting light.

All the pain and grief are over,
Every restless tossing passed;
I am now at peace forever.
Safely home in Heaven at last.

Did you wonder I so calmly
Trod the Valley of the Shade?
Oh! but Jesus' love illumined
Every dark and fearful glade.

And He came Himself to meet me
In that way so hard to tread;
And with Jesus' arm to lean on
Could I have one doubt or dread?

Then you must not grieve so sorely,
For I love you dearly still;
Try to look beyond earth's shadows,
Pray to trust our Father's will.

There is work still waiting for you,
So you must not idle stand;
Do your work while life remaineth;
You shall rest in Jesus' hand.

When that work is all completed,
He will gently call you home;
Oh! the rapture of the meeting!
Oh! the joy to see you come!

Harry Vander Ark

68 THE APPOINTED TIME

Seeing his days are determined, the number of his months are with thee, thou hast appointed his bounds that he cannot pass; Job 14:5

Hans was an active boy who enjoyed high adventure and physical challenges. When he set a goal for himself (or for others), or purposed to do a thing, he often pushed himself to near exhaustion to finish. He did not merely cut brush or put out a fire or rebuild a car. No, these were things that must be *conquered*.

So, it is surprising that he suffered few injuries growing up. A twisted ankle and sore muscles were about the extent of it. The only time he had to go to the emergency room was when he impaled his thumb on a rusty nail.

It is even more interesting when you consider all the dangerous situations Hans found himself in. For a while, he was into snow machines—fast ones; the faster, the better. He enjoyed heading out into the clean, cold winter sunshine and onto the flats, screaming his machine across ice-covered lakes.

And of course, to fill our freezer, he hunted. He once found it necessary to shoot a moose at close range in thick brush. The bullet passed clean through the animal, failing to kill it immediately. We heard the shot from the house. And then another. The distance between Hans and the wounded bull moose narrowed. He fired once more, knocking the moose over backward, but still it was not dead. Wanting to save his last bullet (in case a bear heard the dinner-bell shots), he finished it off with his knife—hand-to-hand combat moose hunting.

There was a time, when he was younger, that I tried keeping a two-way radio on him as he ventured out into the woods to explore his ever-widening boundaries. I liked he could check in with us from time to time. He liked he could radio me when he was starting home, so the food would ready when he got there. But he found it cumbersome carrying a radio all the time, and he finally told me,

"Mommy, nothing can happen to me unless God lets it. Nothing can touch me. I'm totally safe. And then, if something does happen, I go straight to Heaven, so there is nothing to worry about." And he was right, for nothing can happen to us before our appointed time.

Believe it or not, I was not (very) anxious about Hans when he was out in the woods. He was extraordinarily capable, alert and safety minded. But then a brown bear moved into our area, which aroused my concern. Several times, Hans crossed paths with this bear; not necessarily a serious problem if you are carrying a serious weapon. But twice he found himself near this bear while carrying only his .22 rifle. This can be a problem. But even a brown bear cannot touch a boy before God's appointed time.

There were many occasions like this when Hans came close to death or serious injury but escaped completely unharmed. The first time was early in my pregnancy with Hans, when my dad invited me to fly with him to Chalkitsyk. He flew freight around Alaska in those days in a C130 Hercules, which (thankfully) has four engines. Shortly after take-off, one engine caught fire not far from the village. We were never in any real danger, but it surely was an odd thing to happen. My dad told me, in decades of flying in locations around the world, it had never happened to him before.

And when Hans was maybe four years old, Manfred took him along to take measurements on a house located in a small town several hours from our home. This property turned out to be part of a community of women that was into shamanistic healing and rituals.

Some of the locals refer to them as "the witches." They kept a Rottweiler for protection.

One of the women had a young son about Hans's age, so the boys played together while Manfred (quickly) got his measurements. Hans soon realized this little boy needed to hear about Jesus, and so he gave him the simple gospel right then and there. At one point, Hans reached out to pet the Rottweiler and the dog promptly grabbed Hans's hand in its teeth. Thankfully, it let go immediately and the bite was not serious, but the ladies were astonished because the dog had never bitten anyone before. They kindly cleaned up Hans's hand for him, and he and Manfred left.

After he got home, Hans told me about some things the little boy had shown him at this compound. One was an arch made of wood and decorated with big feathers. As Hans approached it, a woman appeared and admonished him not to touch it because the structure was considered by them to be sacred. Perhaps the Rottweiler wanted to make sure Hans's hand *didn't* touch it.

Another close call happened one morning when Manfred was at work. We had some visiting overnight houseguests who were finishing up at the breakfast table with two of our children. An almost five-year-old Hans had just returned from an early trip to the outhouse. He scampered over to the kitchen window, and casually declared, "There's a baby bear on the back porch."

A baby bear means a mama bear. I went to the window and, on the trail leading from the outhouse, where Hans had just walked minutes ago, was a sow bear and a second cub. And she was mad; even from inside the house, I could hear her heavy feet pounding the trail toward us.

Then, there she was, with nothing between her cubs and my cubs, but two thin sheets of glass. She went from window to window, pushing on the glass, trying to get at us. She could hear our commotion (*Get the camera! Get a gun!*) and every sound we made increased her agitation. After what seemed like an awfully long time to an awfully pregnant me, she gave up and lumbered away, her cubs rolling along after her. Relieved, I put the gun away; everyone's cubs were safe.

And then there was the time a pig almost fell on him. We were butchering a hog and had it hanging from a pole between two trees. Hans was busy with some hog-butchering chore nearby when the pig slipped from the pole and came crashing down onto the ground where Hans had just been standing. How would we ever have explained this incident to the emergency room doctor? *A pig fell on him?*

Then there was the crisp blue and gold fall day when Hans was sitting up in a birch tree near our house, surveying his domain. He was minding his own business (for once), when a shot, fired by some careless (and probably inebriated) traveler at the highway rest area, zinged through our yard, shredding birch leaves as it passed within inches of Hans's head. Once again, it was not yet the appointed time for Hans.

And the fires. The last fire Hans assisted with was a wildfire south of Nenana. The fire chief he was riding with took a picture of Hans that day; a framed enlargement hangs in our living room. In the picture, Hans stands atop a U.S. Forestry vehicle wearing his Forestry issued yellow shirt and green pants, a yellow hardhat, a red bandana around his neck, and his trademark "Tom Cruise" sunglasses. His hands are in his pockets and he is looking back at the camera, unconcerned and smiling, as a roiling column of fire consumes a group of spruce trees in the background. *"Raging out-of-control fire, no problem,"* he seems to say. At some point the fire came uncomfortably close to cutting off the firefighters' line of retreat but, thankfully, the wind shifted, and the danger passed.

Then, on January 11, 2016, the winds of Providence shifted again, and Hans's appointed time came. The smiling wildfire photograph from Hans's last summer was displayed with his firefighter's helmet at his memorial service on January 16th. Another print of it hangs in the fire station in Nenana.

There were more potential close calls: a moose that smashed through our windshield on the way to church; an encounter with an arsonist; an excursion across the peak of someone's very steep roof. When considering all the near misses Hans had, I cannot help but wonder: Had the Enemy been trying all those years to eliminate Hans before the appointed time; to take Hans out before he completed the work ordained for him? It would be consistent with that old serpent's evil nature to use things like fire, a pig, a bear, a drunkard's gun, a witch's dog.

But if it was Satan's desire to eliminate Hans early, he was utterly unsuccessful. Satan can do nothing without God's permission; our Lord's perfect plan overrules Satan's schemes. And this I know: God permitted Hans to live long enough to complete every single particle of purpose He had for creating him.

The appointed time comes for all of us. Where will *you* spend eternity? What will you do with Jesus?

> *Come unto me, all ye that labour and are heavy laden, and I will give you rest. Matthew 11:28*
>
> *And as it is appointed unto men once to die, but after this the judgment: Hebrews 9:27*

69 THE NEXT CHAPTER

The father takes his usual place at the head of the table. His wife sits in her usual place opposite him. Their remaining two sons wait quietly in their usual places on his left as his daughter sits down near him, in her usual place on his right. To his wife's left is a vacant chair.

No one openly looks at the chair. He knows his wife probably will, but to avoid her eyes, he does not lift his head to find out. Looking directly at her, right into the eyes, would only reflect and intensify the pain. But the empty chair, like its former occupant, is unavoidable. The terrible silence, the emptiness emanating from the chair, is a smothering heaviness hovering all around them.

Like on a hot day after a train roars by. The train fills your field of vision, drowns out all other sound, threatens to suck you under it, then blows in your face like a bully, and disappears around a bend. It is a deafening wildness, followed by a stark emptiness that leaves only perplexity, the thick smell of diesel and tar-soaked rails in its wake. As it blasts across your path, the train—like grief—is all there is. But the train has passed (for now) and left this jarring silence. Startled, you wonder if it is safe to step across the tracks.

Unopened Bibles wait patiently on the table as if they had lain there for centuries; five Bibles, one for each person. The sixth Bible is up on a shelf next to the bed no one sleeps in anymore. It has been seven days since they have opened the Scriptures together as a family, a whole family. Since the crash, they have prayed together each night as usual before retiring; but reading out loud, reading at all, was more than the father could manage. And now, where in the Word should he turn? Psalms? Maybe select a random passage? He had buried a son that afternoon with his own hands. Are you supposed to just pick up where you left off?

Despite his uncertainty, he senses tonight it is time to attempt some kind of normal. So, he unzips his black Bible cover and opens to the Book of The Exodus—the book of the departure, the going out, the exit. He finds the ribbon that dutifully marks the last chapter they read together two nights before the crash, when his oldest son was still here at the table with them, so strong and alive, and the chair was not yet vacant: Chapter Twenty-Seven in the Book of The Exodus. He glances at the chapter for context and to refresh his memory:

> *In the tabernacle of the congregation without the vail, which is before the testimony, Aaron and his sons shall order it from evening to morning before the LORD: it shall be a statute for ever unto their generations on the behalf of the children of Israel.*

Aaron ministering in the tabernacle of the Lord with his sons. The father's throat tightens. His thoughts flash back to seven years ago when the church building, the entire building, needed new insulation and siding. It was a big job, and he needed to get it done before his regular work season began in the spring. So, in the middle of February, they started ripping off the old wooden siding—he and his oldest boy who was fourteen at the time, his daughter, seventeen, and the two youngest helping where they could.

The worst part was the wind, which would pick up the sheets of insulating foam board and fling them end-over-end down the street. The icy wind in a river town in interior Alaska can make a cold winter day brutal. But the kids never complained, not seriously, anyway.

Working on church maintenance projects was something he and his family found satisfying. It was something they could do together, and he was thankful for their help. Thankful like Aaron must have been when he and his sons ministered together in the tabernacle.

The father's thoughts snap back to the present. Today is the day they move on to Chapter Twenty-Eight of The Exodus—he, his wife, their two remaining sons, and his daughter. He glances again down the page and notices the passage gives detailed specifications regarding the garments to be made for Aaron and his sons. He sees the word *sons* and is not sure he can read the word out loud.

Again, his mind drifts to the past. The memories well up and the threat of tears makes reading aloud, of going on, seem an impossibility. Forward momentum requires strength he does not have. The word *sons* swims on the page.

He remembers the night his oldest son was born, the son who, a week ago, occupied the now vacant chair. He was proud of the boy for just showing up in the world. He remembers him as a little guy, fearlessly handing gospel tracts to people on the street. He remembers his tenacity when faced with a challenge, whether it was learning to ride a bike, unraveling algebra, passing his EMT exam, or rebuilding the car that ended up taking him to Heaven.

He remembers this son occasionally buying lunch for homeless people downtown. He remembers the thoughtful, just-perfect gifts he bought for the family, and how he treated his mother like a queen. He remembers the fishing trips and the firewood cutting, the sledding and the water hauling, and how the only time the boy was quiet for any length of time was when the father would tell a giant story and the son would burrow under the covers with his siblings, mouth open, eyes wide. How good it was when they were all little and Daddy was the center of their universe. Back when everything was still OK.

He remembers the night this son sat in the street waiting for the ambulance to come, with a woman who had just been beaten by her boyfriend, hoping with her that the guy wouldn't come back to finish the job, and wondering what he would do if he did. He remembers how angry the son was to learn there really are men who beat up women.

He remembers this son of his, a young man now, grinning while he helped the father take measurements at a log house they were to chink and refinish. The son holds the end of the tape measure and says, "Daddy, let's make it more expensive." And right in front of the customer, pulls the tape two feet past the corner of the house.

That first work season after the crash, the father kept running out of stain for some reason, though he measured and calculated carefully. It took some time for him to realize the boy had been adding inches all those years to compensate for his father's underestimations. In this way, the son quietly made sure they ordered enough product for each job. It has been two years now, and the father still runs out of product, still underestimates. Underestimating is a hard habit to break.

These are memories the father keeps to himself as he prepares to move forward. There is a final inward groan before continuing; *I have lost a treasure, my Hans, my son. But I am still a rich man; I have two more sons, a daughter, and a wife here with me right now who are waiting for me to take them on to the next chapter in God's Story.*

God help me.

~~~

I say that the tomb that closes upon the dead opens the heavens; and that what we here below take for the end is the beginning;
<div align="right">VICTOR HUGO</div>

70 REMEMBERING HANS

I know of a man and his wife, a little older than my husband and myself, that had a son who died in a car crash. Same age as our Hans, same abrupt end. I do not know these folks personally; they are acquaintances of my husband.

I never met their son. To me, this young man who lived and died many years ago is just a shadow of someone else's past. I do not know his name. I know nothing about him except for the traces of love mixed with sorrow he has left on his parent's aging faces. His family and friends know and remember him, but he is only a nameless, faceless heartbreak to me.

And soon it will be so for us. To the world, Hans is becoming "the son they lost some years ago" and nothing more. New people we meet never knew him. They have no memories of his life, no shared experiences, and therefore they do not miss him.

But I want them to know him. I want you to know our Hans. Then you would know why losing him is so devastating. If you knew him, you would be sad too and you would not wonder why I still hurt so badly. Because you did not know him, you cannot understand. You cannot comprehend the size of the hole in my heart.

If you knew him, you would understand why I sneak his name into conversations. Why I am thrilled when someone speaks his name in a fond, relaxed, and casual way. You would share my sadness because you would be sad, too. But you did not know him. You did not love him. You cannot miss him. You do not remember him.

But it occurs to me, as I think about that other couple's son and acknowledge I did not know him and cannot remember or miss him, maybe I *am* remembering their son. Maybe pondering not knowing who he was, and being sad about that, is a way of remembering him. Perhaps someone thinks the same way about our Hans. Maybe someone is remembering him today.

~~~

A Good Day

"Look at that nose!"

Those were the first words uttered by the midwife that drew Hans into the world. He was ten pounds of vigorous boy, and his mother was simply astonished. After giving birth to a beautiful princess girl almost three years earlier, it never occurred to her she could produce a boy. And she was wonder struck. Her husband took the newborn up in his arms. He seemed to stand a little taller and his chest seemed a little broader with his little son, the *Stamhalter*, bundled up against him. And born on the same day as the little one's grandfather, to boot. His parents were proud of him already and he had not been in the world an hour.

Before leaving for Fairbanks for the birth, we witnessed the sun appearing above the hill near our house for the first time in six weeks. As its rays streamed through our front window, dazzling my eyes, I smiled between contractions and remarked to Manfred, "It's a good day to have a son."

Twenty-one years later (plus a few days), Manfred and I and our two remaining sons climbed into our old red pickup truck. We needed to get the empty, just-finished casket from the church (where it was built) to the funeral home where we would see our Hans for the last time on this earth. As we drove out our driveway past the spot where we would bury him, while the sun shone blearily through the clouds above the hill, I said to Manfred, "It's a good day to bury a son." I did not smile.

No More Hugs

I vividly remember two special hugs that I got from Hans. One was when he was about two or three years old. He was sitting crossways on my lap, and he buried his head under my neck and gave me a wonderful snuggle. Like he just wanted one more extra good one because after that he would be too big to hug his mommy and this one would have to last. It seemed almost a goodbye.

Another was when he was fourteen. We had just had one of those talks that are sometimes necessary when one is fourteen and sparring over algebra. I told him that one of us was going to have to change our approach to the subject; we were both very frustrated. But we talked it out; I told him I loved him, reached up to give him a hug, and we went back to the kitchen table. Oh, how I miss algebra.

Big Plans, Little Time

In the weeks leading up to his departure for Heaven, Hans expressed concern for how we would get along at home without him and Noah. He was preparing to find work in something other than log home restoration, which he had been doing full time (seasonally) for about five years, and part time since he was a little boy. He knew Noah would work with Manfred in just a few months, and he worried that I would have difficulty keeping up with all the chores, with only Josef to help me.

But it was more than that. I could see what really worried him was what would happen when Manfred and I got too old to do the off-grid cabin thing anymore—getting firewood, maintaining vehicles and equipment, etc. I assured him we were prepared to modify things as we grew older, and we would be OK. I reminded him he would always be there for us if we needed him, and we knew we could ask him for help if we needed it.

He did not seem reassured. It was almost as if he suspected he might not be around for the long term and wanted to provide for us somehow before he left. He so wanted to earn enough to help take care of us and to fix up the old home place.

The first thing he wanted to do was to repair our road to give us easier access to our property. He wanted to buy the property adjoining ours and build his home there so I could be a help to his future wife, should the Lord bless him with one. He wanted to build a pond below our cabin and a deck off the living room. He wanted to buy a snow machine for each of us, so we could all ride together.

And he knew, to earn the money for all these projects, he would have to leave us for a while. "But I'll be back," he said, "I'm not going anywhere." I could see he was homesick, though he had not even left yet. I did not really believe he would go. I do not think he did either. At least not forever.

The Car

When you hear that a young man died in a car crash, it is easy to assume he was probably going too fast or driving recklessly. However, Hans was likely moving less than 10 mph when he was broadsided by the pickup. He was a safe, experienced, alert driver and was operating a vehicle with the highest reputation for safety and crash survivability, the Volvo 240. Recently, a stranger was admiring my husband's 1988 Volvo 240 wagon and remarked, "Nobody gets killed in a Volvo." Manfred, rather than disillusion him, said nothing.

Hans's silver and black '83 Volvo sedan was unique in several ways and was a rare find in the United States. The clerk at the hardware store referred to it as a "chick magnet." Hans liked it when all of us crammed into it to go to church: *Check out that heater, Daddy. Are you warm enough, Mommy? Isn't it cozy in here?*

His intention was to have safe and dependable transportation for navigating the challenging highway conditions of interior Alaska. He soon realized it would take some work to restore the car to its full glory, but he was committed to bringing it as close as possible to factory specifications with no hot-rod modification. Hans was a Volvo purist.

He bought it two years before the crash, though most of that time it was parked, undergoing repairs and restoration. He spent hours online searching for hard-to-find parts and worked on it whenever he was not working for Manfred, which mostly meant winter. He would be out there under the hood at 10-20 degrees below zero, in the dark with only a headlamp, wrestling with stiff hoses and stiffer fingers. Once, after spending weeks locating a replacement turbo unit, only to receive one in the mail that had a crack in it, he was ready to quit and just sell the car. We encouraged him to complete the project, if possible, and he did. For you Volvo enthusiasts, I found this on my laptop not long after the crash:

1983 VOLVO 244GLT 2.1L TURBO SERVICE RECORD.
New installations by H. Nolywaika: Turbo, manifold and gaskets, O2 sensor, air filter, all belts except timing belts, thermostat, power steering and brake fluid, all engine sensors except water temperature sensor, PCV hose to air intake pipe, PCV drain hose, PCV gas collection box, oil pump and lower oil tube seal, oil pan gasket, throttle body gasket, ignition switch, vacuum hose t-fittings and all vacuum hoses, both transmission safety nets, converter gasket, cold start injector, idle-air control valve, battery, flushed intercooler, radiator and oil cooler had broken tubes, loose plates and cracked transmission cooler tube fitting fixed on anti-freeze radiator, replaced oil cooler hoses, oil delivery tube for turbo, turbo oil drain hose seal, rebuilt starter and replaced starter solenoid, intake manifold gasket, cleaned entire air intake system, three relays, fuel filter, blower motor, resister and switch, instrument cluster light bulbs, oil and transmission pan heaters, cleaned outside of engine, painted exhaust parts, removed and cleaned inside of oil pan, cleaned transmission pan support bracket, installed turbo waterline kit, had spark plug hole rethreaded, flushed gas tank, turn-signal switch.

There is more, but you get the idea. Hans had two years of his life invested in this car—his final two years, it turns out. It was hard, frustrating work, and I admired him for not giving up. Of course, none of us dreamed he was working doggedly on the car he would die in. It still astounds me. It's like he made the last repair, got in the car, and drove himself to Heaven.

I often think of Hans's final approach to the highway that evening as I drive over those same few hundred feet. I see him proceeding in his car along the same portion of our driveway where he rode his bike as a little boy. I remember waiting with him and our other children, there at the edge of the pavement, for Manfred to come home;

waiting at the very spot where the crash would take Hans from us so many years later. In my mind I see him just driving along, over safe and familiar territory, without an inkling he was taking his last breaths. What was he thinking, those last hundred heartbeats?

About a week after the burial, my husband and I walked up to the highway to see if we could find anything belonging to Hans that may have been ejected from the car. The bright pink spray paint markings were still on the pavement near the end of our driveway but, otherwise, it was nearly impossible to tell that a horrible fatal crash had occurred recently. One set of paint markings followed the left turn Hans made into the path of the pickup truck. The other set of markings circled each spot where his tires came to rest a short distance down the highway. Manfred walked south from our driveway along the edge of the road; I walked north on the opposite side. We were not looking for anything in particular; maybe just evidence that what happened really happened.

I walked slowly, combing the ditch with my eyes as semi-trucks blasted past me, lashing me with a spray of dusty, snowy mist. I hoped no one we knew would drive up and stop, but I truly did not care if passersby thought we had gone batty. As I picked my way through the snow piles, bent over and focusing on the ground, an image from the history books came to my mind of women combing the ruins of a bombed-out city, sifting through the debris, looking for their belongings, searching for loved ones.

But there was no nice Red Cross lady for us today. Manfred and I were alone, alone and together, walking in opposite directions to the same destination. Our hearts were breaking in different places, but they were breaking together.

There was some glass sprinkled in the gravel exposed by the snowplows, but we could find nothing else. We were very, very grateful for the cleanup work done after the crash, but it was still a bizarre disappointment. Hans's car was demolished here and there is nothing lying about to prove it really happened?

I was ready to quit when I saw something shining in the snow. I picked it up; it was the side panel insignia from Hans's car. There in my hand, strangely undamaged and spelled out in cold steel, was eight inches of indisputable proof: *V-O-L-V-O*.

The Road

The dirt road to our house gives us good access in the winter, being frozen hard-pack for six months out of the year. But for the rest of the year, more than a foot of water has often covered portions of it. This has sometimes made it necessary to push a wheelbarrow loaded with groceries a quarter mile to the house, or to wade out to the highway towing toddlers in a canoe while enduring ferocious clouds of mosquitos, or to slog through the mud in our Sunday clothes wearing rubber boots. So, understandably, Hans's first item on his List of Things to Fix (after he made some cash) was the road.

Imagine our astonishment when our pastor notified us, soon after Hans left us for Heaven, that an anonymous someone wished to gift our family with a vehicle for Manfred's business. After thankful consideration, we asked if the donor would be willing, instead, to repair our road up to the value of the new vehicle. We knew the new gift-vehicle would have suffered excess wear and tear, as our other vehicles have, because of the poor condition of the road. The donor was willing and hired a local contractor to fix the road soon after. It was exciting to watch load after dump truck load of gravel filling the low spots in the swamp that we had to cross to get home.

In a note to the donor, forwarded through our pastor, we expressed our wonder and gratitude for this special gift. A quarter mile of gravel is something we never could have afforded, and we let the donor know we viewed this gift as coming from Hans through them and through the provision of Almighty God. Every time I drive down that road, I am reminded of how our loving Father moves people to fulfill His will in unexpected ways. And I know Hans would be thrilled with his new road, the road that God provided.

One Extra Steak

With most of our family working a frantically short Alaskan summer schedule, we did not fish or hunt moose Hans's last year, a serious blow to the meat supply. So, instead, we ordered meat from a local farmer, a whole cow and pig. Hans was eager to bite into that beef—meat acquired without having to slog around in the wet underbrush on a frigid morning.

"I can't wait to eat those steaks," he must have said it twice daily during the weeks we waited for the farmer's call to come pick up the meat. "I want mine rare with plenty of steak sauce. I wish that guy would call." Soon the farmer *did* call—just a few days before the crash.

The last meal I cooked for Hans was the first meal we ate from that meat: pork chops. He never got his steak; not one bite from that cow after all those weeks of waiting. The farmer had custom packaged everything for a family of six. Six steaks, six chops, etc. in each package. So, for an entire year after Hans left us, we had one extra steak, one extra chop. It was strange to see it lying there on the platter at the end of a meal, another silent reminder of the way things used to be.

Memorial Day

Though my father served in the United States Air Force before I was born, I do not come from a particularly military family. Hans did not serve in the military, but, as a volunteer firefighter/medic, he was given firefighter's honors at his memorial service. To be honest, I was floored. I did not expect it and was tremendously thankful and so very proud of my boy.

So, I am now one of those mothers who have been presented with a folded up American flag, something I never in a million years would have thought would be my lot. On this Memorial Day, I want to remember the fallen. I also want to remember the spouses, parents and families who have lost loved ones in service to our country. I want to say, *Thank you.*

Because I know how it feels to be handed that folded up flag.

Citizen of Heaven

Three days before the crash, Hans and I were home, just the two of us. I cannot remember all we did that day—probably just the usual around-the-house stuff. I know he worked on his car and we watched a couple of episodes of *Perry Mason*. But then he hit the off button on the remote. "Let's talk," he said.

He talked about his future and what his options were. He talked about how he would like to make improvements to the house and property. He was concerned about how we would manage without him when he left home. He expressed his dismay at the direction the country was going, the direction the world was going. He talked a lot. I mostly sat and listened.

Then the topic turned to church and the upcoming annual business meeting, which we had asked him to attend. Most years he would wait it out in the fellowship room, playing foosball with the younger kids. He was not planning on sitting in this year; I think he thought, being almost twenty-one years old, that maybe Something Was Expected of him.

"Why should I sit there for a meeting I can't vote in?" He said.

"Become a voting member," I replied. "You've done a lot for the church over the years, but it's time you functioned as a man and not as a boy."

I thought he would get irritated with me for saying something like that. But he just smiled, looked straight at me and said, "I'll always be a boy." And that is just how it turned out.

He went on to question why the church must operate like a business or a republic, with a constitution and voting and members and such. "Can't we just meet and have church?"

I tried to explain that, while the manner in which we structure church government is not ideal, it is the best way we have to protect the church and to make sure we do things decently and in order. He accepted that and was OK with attending the meeting, but he was not ready to commit to membership.

"Why don't you want to become a voting member?" I asked, "Then you could have some say in the decision-making."

"Well, I just don't know where I'll be. When I get settled somewhere, I'll become a member there." That made sense to me and that is just how it turned out the very next day.

His last Sunday on Earth, just twenty-nine hours before the crash, Hans was present for the church's annual business meeting, sitting in his usual place in the second pew, right in front of us and directly in front of the pulpit. On Monday night he was gone.

The Church Triumphant has a new member. Hans is delighting in sweet fellowship, worshipping the Lord in a perfect and glorious assembly where the saints "just meet and have church" and all is love and peace and holiness. Hans is where he is supposed to be.

Last Wish

Three days before the crash, Hans expressed to me that, if there were to be a funeral any time soon in Nenana, he hoped they would call our pastor to preside and deliver a strong gospel message. Not that he hoped someone would die, but funerals are always opportunities to remind people that life is brief and eternity is long.

"Nenana needs a big funeral that Pastor Bob can preach at," he said. Those were his exact words. As we planned the service for Hans, I let our pastor know there was no way I could get through it unless he preached the strong salvation message Hans had hoped for.

And Hans got his wish. Near the conclusion of his memorial service, as I sat in the front row with my heart in shreds, precious Seed was sown as our pastor preached salvation from sin and death, through the shed blood of Jesus. Fighting the tears, I knew at that moment Hans's desire was being fulfilled as the good news of hope in Christ was proclaimed to those in attendance.

After it was over, as I followed the casket out and passed the wildfire photo of Hans, I resisted a powerful urge to turn and give his picture a thumbs up as I walked by. I think maybe he somehow got the message, anyway.

Johannes August Josef Nolywaika
1/12/1995-1/11/2016

But I trusted in thee, O LORD: I said,
Thou *art* my God. My times *are* in thy hand...

PSALM 31:14

Remembering Hans...

From Hans's Memorial Website
http://memorialwebsites.legacy.com/HansNolywaika/homepage.aspx

My memory of Hans is so fun and loving... on earth he was full of love and very silly... I learned a great deal that summer spending time with Kim, Manfred and kids... Hans took me pretend hunting... and we rode stick horses... I am positive he is singing and praising his Savior whom he honored so on earth...

SK

I've been thinking about the little bit of time spent with Hans last summer when he and his dad refinished our logs. For such a young man, Hans made a big impression. It was so obvious he loved the Lord. I could see it in the way he worked, in the way he talked, and in the way he interacted with his dad. He taught me how to use sanding disks on an angle grinder to smooth the logs. A few days ago, I used that training to prepare trim around my windows for painting. It was sad to see such a special life cut short. We had talked about his future plans and I know he was excited for what lay ahead for him. He had no idea a tragic crash would end those plans. I don't know why God wanted him to come home so early, but I do know God does not make mistakes. I still pray for his family as I know there are moments when they really miss Hans. One day they will be reunited in heaven. I know one of the people I'm looking forward to seeing again is Hans. Thank you, God, for allowing me to meet him before you took him home!

CL

Manfred and Kim, some of our warmest memories from our time in Nenana were with your family at your home. I loved watching our young boys look up to Hans with amazement and admiration as he showed them how to take apart and rebuild his pistol. He was always so kind. And smart. And hard-working. I'm so glad we knew him. We had a blast meeting up with Manfred and Hans at Carlos' in Anchorage. And we'll never forget (this is what makes us smile the most) the friendly (and hilarious) banter between Hans and Olivia. We continue to pray for your whole family. We love you all.

R & J

I met Hans back in 2011, when I was living in Nenana. We were in a bible study together and I remember thinking that even though he was still a teenager, he had a passion for Christ and wisdom above his years. He was an amazing young man. When I was around Hans, he usually wanted to talk about snow machining, hunting, or cars. My condolences go out to the Nolywaika family, but I rest in the fact that I will one day see him again.

HY

Although I have never met this young man there are things that I know about him; his love of family, his love for the Lord, his love of friends and community, his commitment in everything he set his hands and heart to. As a consequence of living the beautiful life he led, all of that has come back to you and the family. God gave you a beautiful gift for which there is much pride and gratitude and although God has removed that gift from your sight, for a little while, the gift remains a part of you. All the love he created on this physical earth surrounds and embraces you and holds you close. So close that you can still feel him, smell him, hear him and see him in every gift he left behind for you to hold onto until you are all together again, The sadness and tears although they may overcome you, you know God's promise is true and for that you know that the joy comes in the morning. Praising God for his love and mercy and healing touch.

BN

I had the pleasure of meeting Hans as he worked elbow to elbow with his father as they restored the interior of our log cabin. We commented then "that apple didn't fall far from the tree…. that's Manfred's legacy we're watching". We can only carry a small part of the burden of losing Hans. But we carry it willingly knowing Hans will wait for us, tools in hand and with that movie star smile on his face, when we meet again. Rest easy Hans, we will carry on in your memory. May God bless you and bless you with everlasting peace.

G & S

I visited Manfred at his 50th birthday in 2005 and we went hiking together with Hans. Hans talked much about hiking and the area he knew so very well. We had so much fun together and Hans is for me the same as my own son. He is in my heart... I miss him.

RN

Hans is in so many of my fondest childhood memories. It seems like just yesterday we were eating otter pops in the back of the pickup, working in the hayfields and yelling like banshees at the tourist train, going sledding, having snowball wars. He always let Livvy and I know when he found a good meatwood source, and he chased us with many, many spruce beetles. I hadn't seen him in so long when K's wedding took place. I kept wondering who that tall, handsome, capable looking man was with Livvy... and then realized it was Hans!!! He will never be forgotten. I'm so honored to have known him.

FF

I have lots of good memories with Hans growing up as neighbors. Many a red squirrel was harvested with our slingshots! Whether it was playing down by the creek, making boats, and playing hide and seek and freeze tag, or canoeing in front of the Nolywaika's home, a good time with a lot of laughter was always had! No words can comfort your loss. I have to lean on His promise that our lives here are but a vapor on the eternal timeline. I look forward to seeing Hans again on the other side.

NM

It was a pleasure to know Hans and to spend time watching him grow into a young man who knew the Lord Jesus, followed Him, served Him, and loved Him. We have many memories of your dear son around bonfires, pulling foxtail in the fields, riding horses, pestering the girls while they were "cooking" in their outdoor kitchen, at Christmas and birthday parties... We are thankful for each of you and pray the special closeness of the Lord in each of your lives, for He alone is our comfort and our strength. May you feel His faithful presence even now.

S & R

Hans, we are very sorry that you had to leave us, but I know you met God's calling. I believe you can read this. I remember you from a baby till you grew to be a fine believer in God. I wonder what Heaven looks like to you. We will all in my house miss you until we get there too. Hans, as a father myself, I was very proud of the man you were. I will remember you as a great friend. Tell the Lord we love him too. Hallelujah!!!

BN

Dear Noly family, your friendship means so much to us and we can hardly imagine life without your precious Hans. We know God placed Hans in your very special family to be a very special blessing. We have many fond memories of our years in Alaska: raising our families together, celebrating birthdays and holidays, talking home school, meeting for Bible studies and fellowship, eating yummy homemade food straight from your garden and livestock, surviving harsh winters and basking in summer rays. God has been so good to give us each other, to share in life's joys and sorrows. Thank you for your example of faith in this time of shock and grief. For directing our thoughts heavenward to where Hans now resides with his Savior. Thank you for receiving our condolences and comforting us when your own hearts are breaking. We are trusting you daily to our Heavenly Father for "though he brings grief, he will show compassion, so great is his unfailing love" Lam.3:32. We love you!!

D & B

It's very hard to say goodbye to my grandson. There are no words. I am proud of the man you became; I will always love you. We will see each other again. Grandma.

CV

The first time I saw Hans he was a couple of weeks old. He was a blessing from the very start. I didn't get to be with him as often as I wanted to but when I did get to visit with him he impressed me as being the kind of person we all want our kids to be when they grow up. The last time I spoke to him was shortly before his death. He had always want-

ed to become a pilot. I finally had someone to talk to about airplanes and flying. When Kim called me that evening and told me what had happened, I couldn't believe what she was telling me. The next morning, I hoped it was only a bad dream. I will miss our talks. I was getting to know Hans as a young man who was determined to live out his dream. I love you very much Hans and will see you again. Your Grandpa.

HS

My heart is breaking with this news. Why Hans? Why does the world lose such a kind, intelligent and generous soul? My heart goes out to Manfred, Kim, Olivia, Josef and Noah. I am proud to have known Hans and I am a better person for it. I just spent a wonderful week this last summer with Hans and Manfred at our cabin. They were such a team. Hans worked hard just like his dad and always had a smile or some kindness to say. We spent hours talking about all kinds of things. He was curious and so well educated. We talked a lot about his Volvo which was his pride and joy. Now, when I look at these cabin walls he worked so skillfully and carefully on, I cannot imagine the world without him. This cabin just became ever so much more precious. I am so sorry.

AG

Hans will always be remembered as a nice, well-mannered young man. He was polite to everyone. I will also always remember him for being a prolific reader and all the wonderful educational books that I would get for him per his request. He really had a desire to learn. I am proud to say I was his librarian.

DG

Manfred and Hans refinished quite a few of the log homes I built. I was always impressed by the relationship between Hans and Manfred. The job of refinishing a log home is long and dirty but the atmosphere on the job was always upbeat and cheerful. Then to get in the car and drive an hour back to Nenana together after working that long hard day and do it all over again the next day seemed like a lot to ask from *most teenagers. I could tell Hans was a hard worker and always so polite and respectful. Our thoughts and condolences are with the family!*

BK

Manfred, Kim and family, when I read the e-mail my heart stopped for a beat. Not Hans, please dear Lord not Hans. Hans was a very special human being. From the first time our family met him when he and Manfred came to our home we knew he was special. A young man who was his father's best friend, full of knowledge, laughter, and always spoke of his family. We are so thankful we had the opportunity to spend time with him. While working on our home we became family. My wife would cook dinners for Hans and Manfred; they would sit down for lunch and watch Gunsmoke. We would sit and play the guitar and talk about his dreams of being a pilot. When I saw the Volvo pull up, I was always excited to spend time with Hans and Manfred. We will always have a place in our heart for Hans and his family. God bless you.

LZ

Monday January 11th, 2016, a believer was promoted into heaven. He was a young man and a fellow firefighter and medic. He was saved by grace through faith in Jesus Christ. He comes from a family of believers. The Christian community has experienced hope and joy even in a time of sorrow knowing that we will see this young man again.

Please be in prayer for the Nolywaika family in their season of grief. Also, pray for the fire department. We lost a friend and colleague. We also were the first responders to the motor vehicle collision that resulted in his death. I was one of the medics that had the privilege of providing care for him on the scene.

The funeral was a declaration of his personal faith and an invitation to all present to find salvation in Christ. For believers, we were reminded of our blessed hope and comfort in Christ. The unbelievers were presented with the Gospel and the hope for all sinners who come to know Christ as Savior.

BT

Hans started out in log restoration as a little guy pulling plastic and tape from windows, stuffing it into trash bags, vacuuming decks, cleaning windows, putting tools away, etc. Since most of my work season occurs during the summer months, our kids have helped me on the job since they were very young. Homeschooling has allowed Hans to count his time working with me as vocational training for credit.

Hans started working with me full time when he was fifteen—big enough and strong enough to operate a disc grinder safely. Now barely twenty, he is fully capable of handling by himself any restoration project we might take on. At a time when good help is hard to find, it is great to have a co-worker like Hans who has the same standard of quality as I do.

Hans enjoys photography, hunting and all things outdoors, and is currently restoring his '83 Volvo 240. He recently earned his EMT 1 certification through our local fire department where he and his sister are volunteer responders.

Excerpts from Sashco website: bio:
http://www.sashco.com/marketing/promo/capture/manfred-story.html

Obituary

Johannes (Hans) August Josef Nolywaika arrived safely in the arms of Jesus shortly after six o'clock p.m., January 11, 2016. His departure took place on the Parks Highway near his home north of Nenana, Alaska, after his car collided with another vehicle. He would have been twenty-one years old the following day. Hans was born on January 12, 1995, in Fairbanks on his paternal grandfather's birthday. He was born again on Christmas Eve 1998 in the back seat of a pickup truck while helping his church distribute evangelistic DVDs.

Hans was schooled at home, graduating in 2013. Starting when just a boy, and then full time later on, he worked with his father in the family's business, restoring log homes. Hans was regarded as a hard worker. He liked to do things right and took pride in helping to make the homes he worked on look beautiful. It was important to him that his dad was pleased with his work. Hans honored his father; they were an amazing team.

Hans loved to hunt and roam the woods, often bringing home a fistful of wildflowers for his mother. He loved just being out in God's creation, enjoying the day. He was a competent mechanic and enjoyed aviation, photography, military history, cars, and food. Hans was a volunteer firefighter with Nenana Fire/EMS, serving first as an ETT and then as an EMT 1. His specialty was getting patients (and other medics) to smile.

Hans was blessed all his life by his faithful, praying church family at Nenana Bible Church where he attended regularly. Hans led the singing there for a time on Sunday mornings; he considered the Book of James to be his favorite book in the Bible. He was concerned for the people in his life that do not yet know the Lord and strived to share his faith with those who are in need. Hans was happiest when all the family were home together: repairing something, hauling firewood, sitting by a fire, watching an old black and white movie, listening to music, or just being together. His best friends were his brothers, sister, and parents.

Hans Nolywaika is survived by his parents, Manfred and Kim Nolywaika, sister Olivia Nolywaika, brothers Josef and Noah Nolywaika, Nenana, Alaska; grandmother Carole Vecchione, Delray Beach, Florida; maternal grandfather Harv Schuette, Folsom, California; uncles, aunts, and cousins from Florida, California, North Dakota, Texas, and Germany.

A public memorial service was held for Hans at the Tribal Hall in Nenana, Alaska, on January 16, 2016. A private burial service was held on his family's land near Nenana. He was interred with the ashes of his grandfather, Ernst August Eduard Nolywaika of Reckendorf, Germany (January 12, 1927-December 6, 2013). We will miss his infectious laughter, his boisterous, fun-loving personality, his alert sensitivity, his helping hand. But we thank the Lord Jesus Christ for the solid assurance he gives us that Hans is safe and happy with Him and that, because Hans knew the risen Savior, we will see him again.

Getting Saved in Don's Pickup Truck

It was Christmas Eve, twenty days before Hans's fourth birthday. He and I were waiting in the (very small) back seat for Manfred and Don to return from hanging evangelistic videos on doorknobs in Nenana. We were on the last block, parked in the middle of the street with the motor running and the heater blasting. Hans was unusually quiet. Then he turned to me and said...

Hans (concerned): Mommy, am I a Christian?

Mommy: Well, do you believe Jesus died on the cross and rose again to pay for your sins?

Hans (thinking): Yes.

Mommy: Well then, you are a Christian. Would you like to pray and thank Him?

Hans (fervent and very serious): Yes.

Mommy: OK. I'll go first and then you can pray.

Hans (eager not to lose another minute): OK.

Mommy prays; Hans prays. And another soul is born again, saved and secure for all eternity.

> *Verily I say unto you, Whosoever shall not receive the kingdom of God as a little child shall in no wise enter therein. Luke 18:17*

Let not your heart be troubled: ye believe in God, believe also in me. In my Father's house are many mansions: if it were not so, I would have told you. I go to prepare a place for you. And if I go and prepare a place for you, I will come again, and receive you unto myself; that where I am, there ye may be also. And whither I go ye know, and the way ye know. Thomas saith unto him, Lord, we know not whither thou goest; and how can we know the way? Jesus saith unto him, I am the way, the truth, and the life: no man cometh unto the Father, but by me. John 14:1-6

Jesus said unto her, I am the resurrection, and the life: he that believeth in me, though he were dead, yet shall he live: And whosoever liveth and believeth in me shall never die. Believest thou this? John 11:25-26

Sources

Unless otherwise noted, quotations by other authors are in the public domain and were accessed at the websites listed below. I am indebted to the site owners for compiling, preserving, and sharing these literary and spiritually edifying treasures. Thank you for making the material available; it has brought me much comfort.

Chekhov, Anton. *Misery*. Peterburgskaya Gazeta No. 26, 16 January (old style) 1886. https://americanliterature.com/author/anton-chekhov/short-story/misery

Grace Gems, A Treasury of Ageless, Sovereign Grace, Devotional Writings. https://gracegems.org/

Spurgeon, Charles Haddon. *Morning and Evening: Daily Readings*. Christian Classics Ethereal Library.
https://www.ccel.org/ccel/s/spurgeon/morneve/cache/morneve.txt

Every effort has been made to verify copyright status. Please refer any unintentional infringement to the author. Thank you.

Hans's photographs can be viewed at the author's website: https://youcantrusthim.com/alaskaphotosbyhans/

For Further Reading

Apple, Dennis L. *Life After the Death of My Son, What I'm Learning.* Kansas City: Beacon Hill Press, 2008.

Bruce, James W. III. *From Grief to Glory, Spiritual Journeys* of Mourning Parents. Wheaton Illinois: Crossway Books, 2002.

Elliot, Elisabeth. *A Path Through Suffering, Discovering the* Relationship Between God's Mercy and Our Pain. Ventura, CA: Regal Books, 1990.

Elliot, Elisabeth. *Be Still My Soul.* Grand Rapids, Michigan: Revell, 2003.

Fleece, Isabel. Not by Accident, What I Learned from My Son's Untimely Death. Chicago: Moody Press, 1964, 2000.

MacArthur, John. *The Glory of Heaven: The Truth About* Heaven, Angels, and Eternal Life (Second *Edition).* Wheaton, Illinois: Crossway Books, 1996, 2013.

Wiersbe, David W. *Gone but Not Lost, Grieving the Death of a Child.* Grand Rapids, Michigan: Baker Books, 1992, 2011.

Online Support:

While We're Waiting-Support for Bereaved Parents
   https://www.facebook.com/groups/WhileWereWaiting.SupportForBereavedParents/

About the Author

Kim Nolywaika grew up in New York and Florida before going west at twenty-five. Before her marriage, she worked as a counselor for abused children at a therapeutic wilderness camp in the Florida Everglades, and as a teachers' assistant in San Diego at a private school for troubled children. She headed north to Alaska in 1989 to marry Manfred Nolywaika, whom she met via his personal ad in *Alaska Magazine*. The Nolywaikas enjoy old movies, old cars, old hymns, gardening, good food, and spending time together. They live in a little off-grid log house somewhere south of Fairbanks, Alaska. They have four grown children.

1/11/16, about an hour after the graveside service for Hans.

... I know whom I have believed...
2 Timothy 1:12

Made in United States
Orlando, FL
09 November 2021